Secrets to Catching More and Bigger Bluegill

Let's go catch some slabs!

Table of Contents

Introduction

Section One - The Bluegill
Page 5
General Facts - Habitat - Food Sources - Seasons

Section Two - Tackle & Gear for Bluegill
Page 40
Sunglasses - Poles - Rods - Reels - Fishing Line - Basic Terminal Tackle - Live Bait - Artificial Baits - Prepared Baits - Electronics - Maps

Section Three - Putting Your Tackle to Work
Page 115
Techniques to Catching Big Bluegill
Catching Big Bluegill
Let's Go Fishing

Introduction

Bluegills are a hard-fighting freshwater fish that adapts to most aquatic environments. They provide hours of fishing fun and a tasty meal as a reward afterward. The native range of the bluegill is generally east of the Rocky Mountains in the United States, southern Canada around the Great Lakes, and the north eastern tip of Mexico. Because of their popularity and ability to adapt, bluegills have been distributed throughout most of the United States and many countries throughout the world to be used as a sport fish, forage fish and a renewable food source.

Some consider bluegill a less challenging sport fish because, when the conditions are right, it can be very easy to catch large numbers of them. They will bite on a variety of small baits including: live baits (worms, crickets, grasshoppers and wax worms) and a variety of artificial baits (soft plastics, crank baits, spinner baits and so on). However, if you chase this fish year round and are targeting big bluegills they can be just as challenging as any other species. And the pull of a giant bluegill on light tackle will get your heart pumping as much as any other freshwater species.

The bluegill ranks second in the United Sates as the most sought after freshwater sport fish. The only fish to rank higher is the much promoted and hyped bass. With millions of dollars of corporate money going to advertise bass boats, bass tackle, bass tournaments and so on, it is no wonder the bass is in the number one slot. The bluegill is second without the benefit of any of this support. It is the people's fish with a quiet following. Often it is the first fish an angler experiences and has launched thousands of avid lifelong anglers. You mention a bluegill above 9 inches and you will get most anglers' attention even if they claim to not target the bluegill. Mention one above 11 inches and you have all anglers' undivided attention.

Bluegills are placed in the panfish category with crappie, walleye and bass. Trying to blindly apply general panfish techniques and tactics to consistently catch a large number of big bluegills is unsuccessful. While these methods may work at times, the serious bluegill angler also needs to utilize specific techniques to catch bluegills due to their unique habitats, behaviors and prey. Contained in this publication is the information to help you catch more and bigger bluegill. Whether you are just starting out or looking to improve your game, there are techniques and tactics that will take you to the next level.

Section 1:

The Bluegill

General Facts

Bluegills are part of the Sunfish family (*Centrachidae*) which includes crappie, walleye and bass. More often than not, the term bluegill is used by anglers to refer the entire genus of *Lepomis* which includes a large number of species with the classical bluegill body types. There are also many regional names for this group which include: sunnies, gills, bream, and stump knockers just to mention a few. All of this has led to some confusion as to what people really mean when they talk about the bluegill. Since this group is so tightly related and shares so many common traits we will discuss the following group throughout this publication as they are the most commonly sought after and grow to be the biggest.

- Bluegill - *Lepomis macrochirus*
- Redear - *Lepomis microlophus*
- Green Sunfish - *Lepomis cyanellus*

The bluegill's physical appearance is a horizontally thin and vertically round body with a small mouth on a short head. The dorsal fin is continuous starting just behind the gill plate line with the front portion being spiny and the later more soft and rounded. The tail is slightly forked and rounded in appearance. The namesake feature is the iridescent blue to black gill flap located above the pectoral fin. The body is olive green blending into a mix of copper, orange and lavender on the sides with slightly darker vertical stripes. The belly is a mixture of red, orange or yellow with the males having more intense colors during spawning season. The size of a bluegill depends on many factors in that body of water including population density but generally grows to an average of 9.5 inches but trophy bluegills can exceed 12 inches.

The Redear, or shell cracker as it is called in the southern US, has generally the same shape and coloration except for the ear flap which has a red edge that wraps around the back portion. They originally were found mostly in the southeastern US from about central Texas to the Atlantic Ocean but have been introduced into many waters given their ability to grow faster and larger than most other bluegill species. The primary food of the redear is snails which gave it the "shellcracker" moniker. They do better in warm calm waters with abundant aquatic plants to support the snail population. Given this food source many anglers rely on live bait to catch this variety but artificial baits will also perform well if presented properly. They are generally harder to catch because of the unique diet and many focus on the spawning season to catch them. Common sizes reached are 6-10 inches with 12-15 inches possible in some areas.

The Green Sunfish has a larger mouth and a darker body. Some scales have turquoise spots and turquoise streaks travel back from the mouth under the eye. They were originally native in the area between the Rockies and Appalachians from the Great Lakes southward into Mexico, but have been widely introduced into other areas due to their more aggressive nature. This trait has led to problems with this species as it will typically out-compete other bluegill species in a body of water and reach a population density that produces stunted fish. Green sunfish are usually smaller than bluegills because of their genetics and over population but they are extremely tough and can be successful in very harsh conditions where few other sunfish species survive. This species rarely exceeds 10 inches in length.

Hybrid bluegills are a cross between a male bluegill and a female green sunfish. This crossed fish possesses the traits of fast growth with more aggressive feeding habits. It results in a larger fish that is more easily caught by the angler making it more attractive to anglers. The downside of this hybrid is the fact that 80% are born male which makes it impossible to sustain a breeding population. It also has the tendency to revert back to the green sunfish. This is more of a specialty fish used for in pay-to-fish ponds or food production.

Some of the other more common species you may have experienced are:

- Pumpkin Seed - *Lepomis gibbosus*
- Warmouth - *Lepomis gulosus*
- Redbreasted Sunfish - *Lepomis auritis*
- Longear Sunfish - *Lepomis megalotis*

Bluegills generally live to a ripe old age of only around 6 or 8 years and are slow growers, as shown in the bluegill growth chart on the next page. Of course these are average growth rates and vary greatly from one body of water to another. Some factors that can affect growth rates include: water quality, population density and availability of food. While predation and angler pressure will affect how many make it to their latter years, population density and the corresponding food availability will ultimately dictate the size individual fish can reach in that population. If the demand for food is too high, bluegills will become stunted in an effort to protect themselves so they are able to survive to continue the species. Removing some of the fish in the population by predation or harvesting by anglers will free up more food to the remaining bluegills which allows them to grow larger.

Because the bluegill's slab sided body type they tend to avoid water that has any current. Where a trout glides easily through current with its torpedo shaped body, the bluegills get pushed around and must fight to move or even remain stationary. They typically do better in ponds, smaller lakes and protected coves and bays of larger lakes. They can also survive in the back waters of slower rivers but do not thrive there. The biggest bluegills are found in nutrient rich ponds and small lakes.

Sexual maturity is reached when a bluegill reaches 3 inches in length, which can be achieved within a couple years. The yearly spawn begins when the water temperature reaches 68 degrees and continues until the temperature rises above 89 degrees, with optimal water temperatures between 72 to 79 degrees. The time of year this temperature is reached will depend on your local climate and the size of the water you fish as small waters warm and cool faster than larger bodies of water. The males move into the shallow areas of the pond and begin to make nests to hold the eggs. The preferred bottom composition for constructing nests is loose sand or gravel. This loose substrate makes it easier for the male to sweep out the saucer shaped nest using their fins and tail to fan out a depression. It also allows good water movement so the eggs are well aerated while they develop. The nest ranges from 4 to 24 inches across and 2 to 6 inches deep and is positioned in shallower areas of the pond of about 1 to 3 feet of water. Nests may be in deeper locations if no suitable shallow locations are available in a pond. The nests are grouped in colonies which many refer to as elephant tracks because of the appearance of multiple large footprints in the water. The big males take the prime locations by force and draw in the best females with a showy belly color display and grunts. The females move from the adjacent deeper water to deposit 10,000 to 60,000 of their eggs for the males to fertilize. Bluegills are not monogamous and females will often deposit eggs in multiple nests to ensure success while males will accept eggs from multiple females as well. After the males fertilize the eggs they remain on the nest tending to and guarding the eggs. They keep the clutch well oxygenated by fanning them with their fins to keep oxygenated water surrounding them until they hatch in 5 to 7 days. The newly hatched fry then remain on the nest for a few days to become acclimated to their new environment. During this time they rely on their yolk sac for energy. Once the yolk sack is consumed, they move out into the pond to start their life independently feeding on zooplankton. The male may remain on the nest after the fry have left in an attempt to mate again should any females remain with eggs. Other times the big males move off and one of the smaller males that had been evicted will quickly take the spot to try their luck late in the spawning season.

Be mindful not to harvest too many of these nesting bluegills. These are the breeding stock of the pond and removing too many of them will have both immediate and long term impacts on the pond. First, it leaves the eggs and fry they were guarding open to predation which will lower the number of bluegill in the population of the pond.

Secondly, it reduces the number of bluegill at the proper breeding size to continue the species and can result in a crash in the bluegill population. Large males present in the population push the smaller males out of the prime nesting areas which gives the smaller bluegills time to focus on feeding instead of mating which ultimately results in larger healthier bluegills in a pond. Males will mate as soon as they are of age if given the chance and the energy consumed in spawning slows the growth rate of the fish. Also, when anglers remove all of the big bluegills, it in effect rewards the genetic trait of smaller bluegill since that is the body type that is surviving and creates an artificial evolution of the fish population where only the small survive. Studies have shown that this is possible and may be happening unknowingly around the country. Please consider this while out catching bluegill. Leaving some big bluegill behind will lead to a healthier bluegill population and better fishing for you in the future.

The bluegill is an important link in the ecosystem of any lake or pond. They start their life consuming zooplankton and are prey to larger fish such as bass, crappie and catfish. As they grow, they move on to target insects and larval fish to support their growing bodies while fewer fish are able to predate on them. As they reach their maximum size range they are able to forage farther away from shore and shelter and eat larger prey. Large insects, minnows and crawfish are high energy meals to keep them growing while only the largest predators in the pond are able to prey on them. The bluegill could be considered the keystone to most pond and lake ecosystems as they move the energy from the microscopic level (zooplankton) to the macroscopic levels (large predatory fish).

Habitat

The definition of habitat found in the Webster's New World Dictionary is as follows: "the region where a plant or animal naturally grows or lives; natural environment & the place where a person or thing is ordinarily found." Bluegills live in the aquatic environment which seems both obvious and simple. But what lies below that calm surface of a pond is much more complicated than it appears. We are used to a fairly flat world living on a plane where the majority of our movements are limited to forward and back, left and right. But in the aquatic environment vertical movements are easily performed. Many of the structures that a bluegill relates to on a daily basis are in the vertical plane and may not be obvious to us right away because of our horizontal orientation. Bluegills also prefer calm water that is void of any current to reside as their slab sides catch any water movements pushing the fish around.

Habitat is comprised of structures that serve many purposes, one of which being security or cover. Structure and cover are terms used and abused by fishermen but they are very important when discussing the fish's habitat. Here is a quick definition of each and how they will be referred to in this publication. Structure is a relatively permanent physical object such as a hump or a rock pile on the bottom of the pond. Cover is an object used for concealment such as structures or less permanent items like a dead log floating in the water or a group of aquatic plants that come and go seasonally. Compound or complex structures are multiple structures within a short distance of each other. This situation is highly desirable to bluegill as these complex structures give them more options within a small area, allowing them to expend less energy moving to the optimal location. It also reduces the exposure risk to larger predators.

Not all habitats within a body of water are created equal. Bluegills have certain requirements and preferences that they seek out to support themselves and live a comfortable life. The four most significant criteria for a bluegill are access to food sources, shelter, calm water conditions and access to deep water.

Vegetation

Aquatic plant growth is the preferred habitat of bluegill. This is important and bears repeating. Bluegills will take advantage of weed beds in any pond, lake or river. More specifically, aquatic plants with stalks provide the best habitat. Aquatic plants provide all four traits the bluegill desires. The plant mass breaks current produced by wind, wave or moving water. Abundant food sources are contained within the aquatic plants as this is an excellent environment for the bluegill's preferred prey to live. The cover the plants provide lets the bluegills get close to their prey, reducing the amount of energy used to obtain their food while it also provides the bluegills a place to hide from their predators. Should they be spotted by a bass or walleye, they can use the stalks as obstacles to shake off the predator as they take evasive measures. By squeezing their narrow body between large clumps of stalks, they can squirt through while a wide bodied bass is either stuck or dramatically slowed down in its pursuit. Lastly is access to deep water. Rooted aquatic plants grow anywhere sunlight reaches the bottom of the pond where the bottom composition is suitable to support rooted plants. This zone where growth takes place is referred to as the littoral zone and extends right up to the edge of the deeper water where the sun cannot reach.

The littoral zone is where the majority of biodiversity in a body of water is contained. It should be thought of in terms of depth instead of distance from shore as it is dictated by how far the sun can penetrate into the water to reach the bottom to promote and support plant growth. Variations in slope and the terrain of the bottom combined will dictate how close to or far from shore this area extends. There may be a dip and rise or a submerged hump that sunlight reaches, where rooted plants are able to grow farther from shore. The depth of this zone depends upon the clarity of the water in that particular lake or pond. Turbid waters with suspended sediment and runoff will block the sun's rays from penetrating deeply. Also, fertile waters may produce algae growth that can block the sun just as effectively. On the other extreme, gin clear water allows the sun to penetrate deeply extending the zone to more of the pond. Bluegills will relate to weed beds mostly along the edges. It is easier for them to move about in this environment yet take advantage of the cover.

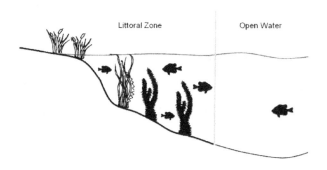

Vegetation is fished in a few ways. The edge along which plant growth starts provides the best opportunity to catch fish. Many predators, including bluegill, position themselves in this area because it is an optimal spot to ambush unaware prey that comes along or emerges from the weeds. Most people are familiar with the deep edge of the weed bed away from shore but keep your eyes moving over the entire area as there may be an inner edge towards the shallows and open holes in the plant growth that can be explored for bluegills as well. Holes are nothing but weed edges that form a circle that can be anywhere from a few inches wide to many yards across. Many baits and techniques can be used to fish these areas such as soft baits, crank baits, spinner baits and live baits. Techniques include casting, trolling, vertical fishing, and bobber fishing.

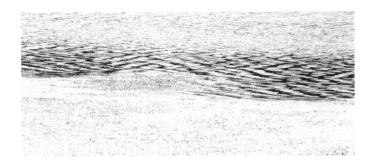

Weed line extending to the surface

Wood

Next up on the bluegill's list of preferred habitat is woody structure. This includes deadfall trees, piers, stumps, docks and other submerged wood. While it does not provide the abundant food source the aquatic plants do, it can have some growth on the surface which supports small organisms. One advantage to wood is that it is a much more solid cover for them to use. If there is any current, this solid structure will break it and create slack water eddies for the bluegills to rest and ambush prey. Also, the bluegill can keep this solid obstacle between them and any predator blocking a strike. The shade created by the woody structure can be fished as a completely separate cover. Hiding in this darker area gives the bluegill a sense of security as it makes it harder for predator and prey to spot them. The shade can also drop the local water temperature a few degrees which will be a draw during the hot summer months. Access to deep water is usually a given with this type of habitat as piers and dock supports extend to the bottom of the pond. Deadfall trees along the shore normally extend out to deeper waters as well.

To fish woody structure you usually have to get as close as possible to the structure which means that you will snag and loose bait rigs. If you aren't at least bumping your bait on the wood occasionally, you aren't close enough to the structure. Start by fishing around the outer areas of the wood structure to seek out bluegill hanging loosely around the wood with soft plastics, spinner baits and crank baits. As you move closer you will have to utilize techniques where you have more control such as vertical jigging or suspending the bait inches above the wood with a bobber. Finally probe the interior of the woody structure to completely explore the center portion to make sure you have exhausted all areas where there may be a potential bluegill. Some of the biggest bluegills have grown to that size by burying themselves into spots like this that have kept them from detection by the average angler.

Open Water

Open water is an area that most do not consider the realm of the bluegill; however, this is where you can often find the biggest bluegill in a pond. Once a bluegill reaches around 6 inches, it is too large for most predator fish in the pond to seriously regard as prey, although the bass has a mouth bigger than its brain and will still try. These larger bluegills will move away from the structure and cover found near shore to the open water in fertile ponds. Fertile ponds can support life in these areas and the competition for food located here is reduced for the bluegill. The big bluegills tend to cruise together in small schools choosing a depth where they are finding the best opportunity to forage. Cover is nonexistent but these individuals use the advantage of being able to see distances to move away from predators before they become a problem.

Open water is more exposed to the effects of wind. During calm weather conditions, bluegill will roam throughout the open water. Should the wind start to blow, they will seek out protected coves or even travel back to shore to escape the waves and current produced.

Open water is best fished by trolling large areas to find the fish. Once located, concentrate your effort near that area as they may be holding there because of a food source or deep structure to which they are relating. Trolling can be accomplished with a boat and trolling motor, in a canoe/kayak or float tube. The wind can also be utilized to push you along, called drifting; it leaves you free to concentrate on your bait presentation and less on boat control. Other than the bait rig choice, speed and depth are the two factors to control and change until you have zeroed in on what is working to get the bite. Many types of bait can be used for this technique such as jigs, spinning baits, crank baits and live baits. Options for techniques to give these baits action are from dead sticking to radical jigging and anything in between. Keep adjusting your presentation until you find the mood of the bluegills that day.

Flats

Flats are wide areas where there is little or no slope. Some are areas where the terrain was flat prior to the formation of the pond or lake while others were filled in with erosion from runoff. They are typically barren areas with mud or sand bottoms but can have a monoculture of plant growth across the expanse. These areas catch the sunlight and warm faster than deeper portions of the ponds, which will draw fish during the spring warm up period. Flats with mud bottoms are also breeding grounds for many aquatic insects and draw the attention of bluegill when the hatch is taking place. The best flats will have cover or deep water nearby for the bluegill to find refuge should predators come into the area.

Fishing a flat is a lot like fishing open water but with a bottom to dictate maximum depth. Approach the area with caution as the bluegill will spook easily given their exposed position. Cover the area as best as you are able with the bait higher in the water column as bluegill usually feed by moving up to their prey. Continue working lower in the water column until finishing with a presentation that is on or near the bottom to fully explore the entire water column.

Points and Humps

Points and humps are topographical structures that will hold bluegill. Points are narrow extensions out from shore that continue into the deeper water. An angler can easily spot these by following the slope of a hill as it continues into the pond. Confirm that this hill extends under the water with electronics or bouncing a jig along the bottom as some slopes drop off suddenly or have been washed away. The ridge that runs out to a point before dropping off into the deeper water gives the bluegill a perch to travel where they can see a good distance while having a structure to use as cover. This provides a safe and easy place for the bluegill to move from shallow to deep water and back.

When fishing a point be sure to explore the entire length and both sides as bluegills will suspend in different locations. Fish it from the outside in, starting out in the deepest waters and slowly moving shallower with each pass so as not to disturb the main school of fish by pulling caught bluegills from the edges. Use the techniques of trolling behind the boat and casting into the slightly shallower areas as you make your passes.

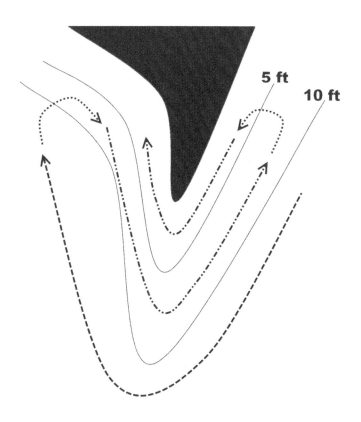

Humps range from a submerged island in the middle of a lake to a small group of rocks piled on a flat. They function as isolated points that give the bluegills structure to relate to in an area that provides them with little other cover. Again, fish the humps from the outside in to the shallowest section. Pulling fish from the edges keeps the school in a more calm state making it easier for you to catch more bluegill.

Channels

Channels are narrow depressions in the bottom terrain such as old stream beds that have been covered by water as the pond was filled with water. These old streams once led downhill so now they have become underwater highways that connect the shallows to the deepest portions of the pond. Not only are they a path to follow but they also provide some cover as the fish moves. Some channels are deep cuts where a bluegill can find places to hide from predators and unfavorable conditions. Other channels have been filled in with sediment over time and are more of a shallow depression that fish simply use as a structure to relate to as they move. You can find these features by observing where current streams enter the pond and confirm their depth and direction with your electronics or by bumping the bottom with a jig.

Fish the channels by moving your boat along its path while probing around and inside. Deep cut channels can hold fish year round because of the cover they provide, while shallow channels are more seasonal transition pathways. Channels have the most activity in the spring and autumn when fish are on the move to or from the depths.

Transition Zones

Transition zones are changes in bottom composition such as from mud to sand. This change in the bottom is a subtle structure for the bluegill to relate to in areas without other forms of structure. These are sometimes hard to find and may require electronics or knowledge of that body of water. Attentive fishermen can pick up on small indicators and confirm these with a jig to feel the bottom or electronics that show a difference in the reflectivity of the bottom composition.

Fish the transition zone along the length as you would fish a channel. Finding the exact line is difficult, so zig-zag along the area and you will cross the transition line multiple times as you fish. Since bluegill do not hold tight to the exact line, you will fish the area more thoroughly and catch more bluegill.

Steep Banks & Bridge Pilings

While they provide very little cover, steep vertical structures do provide the bluegill with benefits. These areas obviously provide easy access to deep water, allowing the bluegills to move effortlessly in the water column while providing a current break giving them a place to rest. The surfaces are typically rock or riprap that catches and transmit the sun's warmth down into the water creating a warmer local temperature that is desirable when the water is cold. Other structures in conjunction with a steep bank make it a very attractive location as a deadfall tree, weed line or hump will give the bluegill cover while providing all of the other benefits.

Fish these structures like a point or hump. Start out away from it and in the deeper waters while moving gradually closer and shallower. Pick off the aggressive fish on the fringe and move into the less aggressive bluegill holding tight to the structure.

Artificial Habitat

One type structure that can be very important and even change the productivity of an entire pond is artificial habitat that is placed into the water. This practice has been in use for hundreds of years to draw in fish to a known location with good results. Placement of these structures can serve to expand current habitats or create entirely new ones in previously barren areas. Many anglers choose to create their own habitats using commonly available materials such as deadfall trees, old Christmas trees, pallets, tires and even old milk jugs combined with PVC to make "trees". Manufactures have recently gotten into the act as well with a variety of structures of different shapes, sizes and materials.

Only consider placing artificial habitats if you own the pond or have written permission from the land owner. Placing structures can be dangerous to users of that water should someone else be using the area to swim or dive into the water while unaware of this new hazard. Also, make sure you are very familiar with the materials that are being used for the structure. Some materials may give off toxic compounds into the water that can negatively affect the fish or people in the area.

Structure placement is best done in sets of three to five with gaps of 6 to 8 feet in between. This creates a chain similar to a fresh water reef that fish can move along. One artificial habitat placed alone may not be enough to draw in the bait fish for the bluegill to forage on while clumping the strucutres too close together does not allow for predators to be able to feed and they will not make it a location they visit often.

Stratification and Thermoclines

One factor that is sometimes forgotten that can dramatically affect the habitat of the bluegill's world is stratification. This is an event where two masses of water form in a pond with a thermocline preventing them from mixing. Oxygen rich water will remain on top while the water trapped on the bottom becomes devoid of oxygen and toxic to fish.

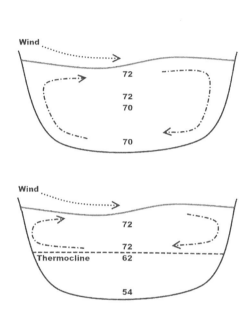

The thermocline in effect becomes a floor which fish will not pass under. Depths of the thermocline vary depending on the body of water and the conditions which caused it to form. It typically occurs during the calm summer and winter months and does not happen in every body of water as ponds of less than 10 feet deep are less likely to experience this phenomenon.

In the spring and fall, the pond will experience what is called a turnover. As the air temperatures change, so does the temperature of the upper layers of the pond until the upper and lower layers come close enough together that they can again mix. It happens quickly and with vigor which stirs up the water and gives it a turbid appearance with no obvious cause. When these two masses mix, the overall effect is that the oxygen level of the entire water column drops and the toxins are distributed throughout the entire water column from the waters trapped at the bottom. Bluegills are typically in the shallow reaches of the water column and the only time stratification affects them dramatically is during a turnover event. Fish may become inactive or even suffer a fish kill when this occurs. Laminar flow aeration of private ponds is one method of preventing this from stratification.

Habitat Summary

The habitat of the bluegill is wide and varied as they are a tough and adaptable fish that can find opportunity in most niches of a pond, lake or river. Bluegill have a preferred habitat, of nutrient rich calm waters containing stemmed aquatic plants adjacent to deep water access, but will take advantage of any type of habitat and cover they can find with a good food supply.

As young fry, they remain buried deep in the thickest cover to protect themselves from predation while foraging for food. Their range grows with their physical size as fewer fish are able to prey on them and they can take chances moving out into the more open water where it is easier to move and hunt for their food sources. The biggest bluegills will be found further from shore and in smaller schools as they seek out the largest and most nourishing prey available to them. By focusing on the preferred habitats of the bluegill you will put yourself in the right location to catch more and bigger bluegill.

Food Sources

Bluegills are famous for their small mouths and big appetites. They are opportunists that will feed on about anything they believe to be a food item and can fit into their mouth. At times, such as in the spring, they are like fresh water piranha ripping at anything that passes in front of them. At other times of the year, they are more selective and cautious about what they attempt to consume.

As a bluegill starts its life as a fry it feeds on what almost every species feeds on, zooplankton. Zooplankton are tiny creatures that feed on phytoplankton and are a great energy source for a growing body. In addition, zooplankton reside in tight cover where the bluegill fry can find a safe harbor from the larger predators that are seeking them out for food. As the bluegill grows, so does its mouth and appetite. Their diet expands to include aquatic worms and other aquatic invertebrates that reside in and around the weed beds they use for cover. As they reach the 6 inch mark, fewer predators are able to target them and they become bolder and begin to target the eggs and new born fry of other fish species. Bass eggs and fry are a favorite target simply because they are usually the other most prominent fish in the pond. Consider it karma for the bass constantly hunting down the bluegill throughout its entire life.

Zooplankton, insects, eggs and fry comprise the vast majority of the bluegill's diet for most of its life. If a bluegill is lucky enough to live to a ripe old age of 6 years or more and attain the size of over 8 inches, it can add even more to its diet. This is when large insects, minnows and crayfish are all fair game. Whether the insects are blown in from the shoreline weeds or using the water as part of their life cycle, they are a seasonal boon to supplement the bluegill's diet. And don't forget the Redear which specializes in eating small snails and mollusks for the bulk of its diet. A short list of potential food sources can be found in table 1.

Consider these food sources when choosing the baits you plan to use whether it is live or artificial. By matching the preferred food sources when using live bait or generally matching those with an artificial, it will greatly improve your odds of success. Also, while tiny baits may produce greater numbers of bluegill caught, larger baits presented in the right places will produce bigger fish. Once you have located bluegill in a pond, sizing up into a larger bait rig will often produce a larger bluegill.

Table 1:

Potential food sources of the bluegill

Aquatic Worms
       Aquatic earthworm (Oligochaete)
       Nematode   Planaria

Crustaceans
       Copepods (zooplankton)   Crayfish
       Ostracods (zooplankton)   Water fleas (zooplankton)

Insects (adult, nymph and larvae)
       Caddisfly   Dragonfly
       Fly   Mayfly
       Mosquito   Stonefly
       Riffle beetles

Mollusks
       Clams   Limpet
       Snails

Vertebrates
       Fish (eggs and fry)   Frog (eggs and tadpoles)
       Minnow species (chubs, shiners, etc.)

Other
       Anything that will fit into their mouth or can
       be pulled apart to fit.

Seasons

As the seasons change, so does the location and attitude of the bluegill. As with any animal, the seasons will dictate what is available to eat, what cover is available to utilize, and what conditions the bluegill will face. Bluegills move throughout the water column over the year to find the location that provides them with the best conditions to survive. By knowing how the bluegill moves during the seasons and what the primary focus and attitude will be, you can achieve greater success in your fishing endeavors.

Winter

The winter is a slow time for the bluegill as food is scarce, habitat is reduced and water temperatures are cold. Their goal is to make it through the hard times until spring brings bounty again. Conditions are brutal with water temperatures being as low as the mid 30's. The coldest waters are located near the top of the water column close to the ice and the warmest water near the bottom of the pond. Cover is very limited with most plant life being dormant for the season and only inanimate objects such as rock humps, points, channels and deadfalls still available. Food sources are very limited and predators are on the prowl for a meal to get them through the tough times as well.

Oxygen supplies can also dip during the winter months, compounding the problems for the bluegill. Filamentous algae will continue under the ice on or near the bottom of the pond producing oxygen throughout the winter. However, a heavy snow or cloudy ice formation can block the sunlight which reduces oxygen production and may even lead to killing off the algae if enough light is blocked. Should the algae die the oxygen production is obviously ended but then the decomposing vegetation will consume the oxygen remaining in the water creating an oxygen crisis which can result in a fish kill. Private pond owners can prevent this series of events by removing the snow from the top of the ice or installing an agitator which keeps the water open, allowing sunlight in and oxygen transfer between the water/air surfaces.

Bluegills will keep their movements to an absolute minimum during this time to preserve their energy. They seek out the warmest water with food and cover and stick close to that location. Deep water with wood structure usually is a good place to start looking for them. Woody structure such as standing trees that come above the surface of the water are able to absorb and radiate any heat gained from the sun into the surrounding water below. If there is a lack of one good location to gather, bluegill will school together and slowly cruise the depths in search of food while using their numbers to protect against predator attack.

Spring

Spring brings about big changes and better times after the tough winter. The water opens up and increases the oxygen content and the water temperatures. The bluegills will seek out the warmest areas. Early in the season, structures rising out of the water will transmit warmth down into the water as they absorb the sun's rays and bluegill will be drawn to those locally warmer waters. North shores are also good places to find warm water as they catch the most sunlight in the lengthening days. If they are covered with riprap, they become even more of a heat conductor and should be targeted for fishing. Flats and wood structure near the surface are also heat sinks that draw a crowd of bluegill.

As the water warms, more and more prey are available to the bluegill and they eat voraciously to gain back their strength and prepare for the spawn. They will utilize cover such as channels, weed lines and points to move up from the depths into the shallows where the water is warming up and life is coming back.

Mid to late spring brings the beginning of the spawning season. As the water temperatures reach the lower 60's, the males move up into the shallows and select sites for creating a suitable nest in preparation for the spawning event. The biggest males push out the competitors to get the best locations. They will create colonies of nests in 1 to 3 feet of water where the bottom composition is sand or pebbles and there is access to deep water. They prefer this bottom composition, as it is easier for them to form the nests using their fins to fan out a depression. Also, this material allows the eggs to have good water circulation keeping them aerated and healthy. Silt or mucky bottom composition will smother and kill the eggs. The females congregate in the safe deeper water adjacent to these spawning beds until the conditions are right for spawning. When the water reaches the mid to upper 60's, the females begin moving into the nesting area to deposit some of their eggs into a nest. The males fertilize and tend to those eggs by protecting them from predation and fanning them to keep them well aerated until they hatch in about a week. They continue to protect the hatched fry as they remain close to the nest while the yolk sac is used and they get acclimated to their environment. Only after the fry have moved out into the world will the male abandon the nest. Spawning peaks between 70 to 75 degrees but will continue even slightly above and below this range.

Depending on the location and climate, the spawn will continue for weeks and through multiple cycles while the conditions are in the optimal range. Female bluegills do not deposit all of their eggs the first time they visit a male's nest and will retain a portion of them to spawn again later in the season. This may be a defensive strategy to insure some of their offspring survive in case bad weather or predation destroys the first clutch. In the south, spawning can cycle for 4 to 6 times, the Mid-west 3 to 5 times and the north 1 or 2 times due to the shorter seasons.

During the entire spawn the bluegills are burning an incredible amount of energy and seek out food accordingly. There are many options available to them at this time of year including aquatic insects, aquatic worms, fish eggs, fry, small crawdads and minnow species. Even after the spawn, the bluegills typically remain near the shallows where the food supply is high and cover is plentiful as the rooted submerged and floating plants are growing rapidly. During steady weather, they will be aggressively pursuing food.

Summer

As the summer heats up so does the water. The shallows where the bluegills took up residency in the spring may now become too warm for them to comfortably forage for food. Life is at its peak in the pond and bluegills have many opportunities to feed throughout most of the upper layers of the water column. While small bluegills will remain in the shallow cover to forage and for protection, larger fish will move into deeper water where temperatures are more favorable. Deep weed lines and woody structures are magnets for bluegill as they are in the cooler water yet provide cover for them to avoid predation. Large bluegill will move out into the open water and forage if the water is nutrient rich enough to support forage in those areas. There are some shallow areas that will remain cool and will retain bluegill such as shaded areas under trees or in an area with thick lily pad growth blocking out the sun.

Bluegills will be active in the summer but may curtail their activity when the water gets too warm for them to be comfortably active. Some ponds suffer from oxygen depletion at this time of year which will cause the bluegill to be inactive until oxygen levels come back up to normal. Search for cooler water even if it is only a few degrees as it can be enough to make the difference for an overheated bluegill.

Fall

Fall begins the cool down period and kicks the action back into high gear. The cooler temperatures and decreasing daylight is a signal that winter is making its way back and that it is time for them to feed heavily to store up as much energy as possible before the hard times set in again. As cooler water moves back into the shallows, bluegills follow to take advantage of all food sources available during this time.

Bluegills are generally more aggressive throughout this season and will move between the deep and shallow areas to maximize feeding opportunities as the weather changes. Autumn is one of the best kept secrets of avid anglers as many hang up their fishing gear to go hunting, watch football or pursue other seasonal activities. One can find themselves all alone on a lake catching bluegill in the cool crisp autumn air. It is pure bluegill paradise.

The Seasons

Bluegills, like all animals, take cues from the environment and move to optimize their chances of finding food, shelter and to be in the most comfortable water. While weather and timing of the seasons vary from year to year, bluegill will follow the cues rather predictably. They typically are in deep water in the winter and summer, while in shallower water and becoming more aggressive in the spring and autumn transition months. Before you head out on the water, consider the time of year, the recent weather conditions and where they are likely to be. Start at those typical locations and branch out from there to find fish faster. You will get quicker results and will then be able to fine tune your presentation to catch the big bluegill.

Section 2:

Tackle & Gear for Bluegill

Now that we know the habitat the bluegill prefers, the food sources they typically target and some of the seasonal movements within a body of water, let's shift our focus to what it takes to catch these freshwater "piranhas" on a consistent basis. In this section we will review what gear and tackle is needed for a successful day on the water in pursuit of big bluegill.

Sunglasses

This is a piece of gear that is critical to your health as well as improving your fishing. Sunglasses protect your eyes from the glare that you will be exposed to for the entire time you are on the water, even as you drive to your favorite fishing spot. You will be exposed to more sunlight than the average person because you are getting both the direct sun from above and reflected light from the surface of the water. And don't be fooled on a cloudy day, there is still a large amount of glare reaching your eyes. This glare prevents you from seeing into the water and over time damages your eyes irreversibly.

Most of the glare we experience is in the horizontal plane; whether it is bouncing off of a car hood, a snowy field or the water's surface. Polarized sunglasses are designed to remove light oriented in the horizontal plane and are the sunglass to wear the entire time you are fishing. With the horizontal glare removed there is less strain on your eyes and you will be able to see deep into the water. Sunglass manufacturers claim that you will see 50% more underwater detail with a pair of polarized sunglasses. The difference is amazing. You will be able to see the bottom structure, weed lines, your bait as your bring it in and fish as they move through the water.

Many manufactures produce polarized sunglasses with a wide range of costs. You don't have to go crazy here but I recommend sticking with a company that had fishing in mind when designing their sunglasses as they will have features meant for anglers. Wrap around lenses are the most comfortable and provide the most protection as they block unfiltered light from entering from any direction completely sealing your eye from harsh light. Another good feature to have in sunglasses is a vent system above the lenses as fogging can be a problem. While cost does not guarantee better sunglasses it usually does indicate a better made product.

Sunglasses come in a variety of colors such including amber, brown, copper and gray. Amber and copper lenses are meant for low light conditions such as sun rise/set, overcast skies and when fishing in the shade. These are the best for shallow water fishing. Amber increases contrast which gives the angler better depth perception. Copper improves the distance you can see under the water and gives you slightly better clarity. Brown lenses are the best all around lenses because they are color neutral. This means brown reduces overall brightness without distorting colors. Brown works best in moderate to bright conditions and is the best choice if you prefer to purchase and use one pair of glasses for all light conditions. While the contrast is not as good as amber and copper lenses, they work over a wider range of light intensities. Grey lenses are best for very bright sunny days and when fishing deeper water. Gray dampens bright light without much color distortion and will give your eyes the most comfort over a long period of time.

Style, color and fit are all personal choices, so try out a few lower cost options for yourself before you invest in a more expensive pair. But make sure you do buy and wear a pair of polarized sunglasses every time you head out to fish. Your experience fishing will be better; your eyes will be less stressed at the end of the day and healthier in the long run.

Poles

The fishing pole is the original tool that increased a human's reach as we pursued fish. It allowed us to get our baits out into the water and control placement. The fishing pole was a fairly simple piece of equipment with a static line attached to the end of a stick. For years cane poles were the standard, providing the angler with segments to extend the pole out as far as required getting to the spot. While cane poles are still on the market, new poles are made of very modern materials such as graphite, fiberglass and composite materials. Some have reel mounts but others have more simplistic line keeper clips to store line near the butt of the pole. Some are fixed in length but others have a telescopic feature that allows the angler to adjust the pole for an exact reach.

The action imparted on bait with a pole is limited as the line is static and cannot be reeled in on most models but the pole's reach allows for a stealthy and accurate presentation. Bait rigs can be placed and fished with delicate precision and in exact locations. This subtle presentation can be the difference when bluegills are inactive or skittish. It can also open up fishing spots that cannot be reached by boat or by casting with a rod and reel combo. Placing bait into a hole in a thick growth of aquatic plants rather than plowing into the area with a boat will catch more fish. Also, dropping a fly onto the surface of the water at a distance is much easier with a pole than casting with a fly rod, especially in the wind. They are relatively low cost and are a piece of specialty equipment that any angler should consider adding to their arsenal. And since many collapse down to a very compact size they are easily stored in a boat, car or garage.

Rods

The rod and reel combination is usually what people have in mind in the U.S. when they think of fishing. Rods come in spin casting, spinning and bait casting styles. They have the proper mounts for these various reel choices near the butt with foam or cork handles.

The two significant features of a rod to consider are the action and power. The action refers to the how much of the rod flexes when a fish, or load, applies pressure to the tip of the rod where the line comes out of the last guide. Slow action rods bend for most of the length of the rod to almost the butt where the reel is mounted in the lower $1/3^{rd}$ of the rod. It takes more time to bend this entire distance hence the nomenclature of slow action. Fast action rods bend mostly near the tip of the rod in the top $1/3^{rd}$ of the rod with a quick motion. The power of the rod describes its stiffness or resistance to bending. Powers are heavy, medium, light and ultra-light. Heavy rods are made from more rigid composites and are generally thicker while ultra-lights are made of less rigid composites and are generally thinner. Heavy rods are designed for heavy tackle and thick line and do not serve our purposes. For bluegill, the lighter powered and fast actions rods are the best. They are able to cast the small baits, handle the lighter line and give us the best feel of the bottom and the bite as we fish.

The term "feel" refers to the vibrations sent up the line, transmitted to the rod and ultimately your hand as you fish. These vibrations can let you know the bottom composition and structure present as the bait jig drags over and bangs into them. The feel is also very important when a fish is biting or nibbling at your bait. If you cannot feel the fish, you will miss the hook set. You can learn the feel of various objects by gently dragging your bait over an obstacle you can see in the water. Now you will know what that object feels like with that bait, rod, reel and line. Try this with rocks, stumps weeds and anything else commonly found in those waters. Then if you feel anything that does not match those items, IT'S A FISH!

Lengths of rods range from around 4 feet to 12 feet or more. Each has it purpose but a good all around bluegill rod is a fast action 6 ½ foot rod with light power. Shorter rods tend to be better for casting accurately while longer rods are better for longer casts due to the energy produced by the large casting arc. Many anglers go with the ultra-light power for bluegills thinking that it performs better with the light weight baits. I have found through experience, and backed with discussions with other anglers, that the light power rod is actually better at casting these light weight bait rigs. The ultra-light rods waste a lot of energy with a whipping action that does not focus the bait out for a long cast. Also, light bites can be missed as the ultra-light rod does not transmit the vibrations as well. Again, energy is lost in the noodle-like core of this rod. The light action rod has a little more backbone to focus the energy of the cast to launch the bait out a good distance, even into a wind. The slightly increased rigidity also gives a better feel. This rod also handles heavier baits and crank baits with ease making it a better choice for using in most situations.

Fly fishing rods are a specialty rod that casts ultra-light micro-baits. When fly fishing, one casts the line and the bait follows. Most of the flies used for bluegill are fairly small, so a rod in the range of a 3 weight is a good choice. Longer fly rods make casting easier in open areas while shorter rods are better for a spot that has thick growth such as trees and bushes on the shore.

Ice fishing rods are just much shortened versions of a standard fishing rod. Most are fitted with spinning reel seats or very simple line holding spools. You will never cast one of these so the most important consideration is the feel and power to set the hook and bring the fish to the surface. A fast-action light powered rod will give you the hook setting power you will need for bluegill while flexing enough to protect the tiny 1 to 2 pound test line that will be used during ice fishing season.

Starting with a good all around rod will allow you to get going without investing a pile of money on multiple rods that you have to drag around when fishing. As you fish, you will learn your style and can then invest in the specialty equipment to fit your needs and then just take what fits for that day's expedition. Don't cheap out on the rod. It is a critical part of the puzzle and you will be able to use a good one for years if not decades. More expensive rods have better composition material, better guides, and better reel seats and therefore better performance. You do not have to run out and purchase the most expensive rod on the market, but a mid-ranged rod will greatly out perform the discount store variety.

Reels

The reel is designed to hold your line when casting and when bringing in a fighting fish without putting undue stress on your line. A smooth running and reliable reel will keep you going through the entire day while a cheap unreliable reel can completely destroy an otherwise good day of fishing. Consider the manufacturer and inspect the reel to make sure it is a solid product that will take the abuse of banging around in your garage, car and boat before it even makes it to the water. Smooth reeling action and a good drag are critical features no matter the style.

Spin Cast Reels

What many people started their fishing career with is a spin cast reel. It is a closed face reel with a distinctive push button on the

back. You simply press the button down, flick the rod forward and release the button just as you reach the forward position. The energy of the rod then propels the bait out into the water. With a simple turn of the crank, the internal bail closes and the line is secured to set the hook to catch fish. Drag is adjusted with a small wheel on the side or top of the reel. These reels are mounted on top of a pistol gripped rod and handle bluegill wonderfully. They are great for beginners to learn the proper casting technique as you can pick up the motion in minutes and can be fishing immediately. There is a misconception that they are only for novices and children, but this type of reel has come a long way and technology has improved this reel as much as any other. While they are typically the most inexpensive reels, they will do a great job for you. Look through your options and the features of each reel on the market. Ball bearings make the reel run smoothly and generally speaking the more ball bearings in the reel the smoother the operation. In general the drag systems are less reliable than other reels and they have less line capacity, but they are still a great reel for bluegill fishing.

Spinning Reels

Spinning reels are the most used reel for bluegill fishing. They are the open faced reel with a large wire bail that hangs on the bottom of the rod. The bail is opened to release the line to cast. This is accomplished by either opening the bail manually or with a trigger type opening system on some models. I recommend using the manual models without the opening system as these systems have many tiny moving parts and springs that can fail at the worst possible moment. No time is lost opening the bail with your free hand while fishing and once you get used to the motion it becomes an automatic habit you don't even realize you are doing. Just pinch the line to the rod with your index finger, open the bail and cast while releasing the line. The bail moves completely out of the way when casting, eliminating friction which enables even the tiniest baits to be sent  farther and with more accuracy than any other reel. Then comes the most important part of the cast, close the bail WITH YOUR HAND. Turning the crank to close the bail will cause line twist which these reels are already prone to do. Save yourself the headache and get in the habit now. The drag system is more advanced than the spin casting reels and the line capacity is much higher so you do not have to spool on new line as often. These reels can handle line from the lowest pound ratings to the highest depending on the size of the reel. A smaller reel will match up with a light or ultra-light rod and handle the light line and baits that we are using.

Gear ratios indicate line retrieval speed and are based on the number of times the bail rotates around the spool per turn of the crank. The higher the ratio, the faster the line is being brought into the reel. A 5:1 means that the bail travels around the spool 5 times for every 1 full crank and so on for 4:1 and 6:1. So the speed that bait is returning to the reel depends on the ratio and the diameter of the spool. A ratio of 4:1 is considered slow while a ratio of 6:1 is considered fast. The 5:1

ratio is a good compromise should you be interested in purchasing only one reel, as it will bring in crank baits quick enough to impart action and you will be able to slow down the cranking enough for slower baits.

When it comes to smooth operation, stability and durability, ball bearings play a large part. Most good reels will have a minimum of 4 to 6 bearings while top of the line reels will have up to 12. I recommend never going below 4 bearings as you will sacrifice performance and ultimately enjoyment. After that, it is a matter of personal preference.

Always check the drag system when purchasing. It should operate smoothly and consistently without any hesitations. There are two drag systems available for this type of reel and I recommend the front mounted drag as they are more reliable and smoother in operation. The rear mounted drag offers you access to adjust the drag while fighting a fish but are less reliable. Anyway, you should never be adjusting your drag while bringing in a fish as it should already be set to the proper level prior to fishing. The front mounted drags use large multiple washers that are more durable and dependable.

Spools are made from many different materials and in slightly different shapes. These variations are all intended to increase casting distance. You will have to research spools available in the market at the time you are looking to purchase your reel as technology and trends keep changing. Much like the computer industry, what is cutting edge today is outdated tomorrow.

The anti-reverse function of the chosen reel should activate immediately upon reversing direction or stopping the crank. Some reels only have a stop at one point in the rotation of the bail while this seems to be a minor issue until it results in lost hook sets. If the bail happens to be in the wrong position, it creates a large slack area where the bail is not locked and line spools out as you thrash to create tension on the line. The immediate engaging anti-reverse allows the angler to have instant control over the line and set the hook faster.

Bait Casting Reels

Bait casting reels are the last reel to be discussed and the discussion will be short. These reels have an open horizontal spool and sit on top of the rod. When you cast, you must hold the spool with

 your thumb while you release the brake to prevent it from spinning freely. As you move the rod forward you release the pressure on the spool to allow line out while casting but then have to reapply when the bait hits the water and stops. Failure to do so will result in what is referred to as a bird's nest. It happens when the spool continues to spin out line after the bait has stopped taking line out and it turns

into a mess on the spool and the tangles are a nightmare to remove. These reels are designed for heavier line, rods and tackle that we will not be using. Small scale versions of this reel have come and gone from the market and just do not work well for our purposes.

Fly Fishing Reels

Fly fishing reels are not a major consideration when fishing for bluegill. Most of the time you will not be utilizing the reel to bring in the fish as stripping the line is much more efficient than trying to engage the reel. A good basic reel is enough for most bluegill situations as it serves as more of a line storage unit that anything else.

Adjusting the Drag

One last point to discuss in the reel section is how to properly adjust the drag as it is very important in setting up your reel. Too high of a setting and you will break off every fish you hook. Setting it too low and the fish will run forever and possibly wind your line onto a tree branch or other cover.

I used to set the drag like the old timers taught me. Crank up the drag until it just barely comes off the spool before breaking while pulling line out just above the reel. I have learned over the years a better method that results in fewer break-offs while giving control over the fish. Allow several feet of line to hang out from the tip of the rod.

Adjust the drag so that when you pull on the line coming from the tip of the rod, it will slowly come off of the spool. This method better mimics the pull of a fighting fish loading the rod and I believe allows you to more accurately adjust the drag to the tension that the fish will actually be putting on the line. The goal is to set the drag so that it relieves the pressure of the fish slightly below the breaking point of the line. While the fish we seek are small, our line will be very low in pound test rating and you do not want to risk losing that record bluegill. When you get a ten or twelve inch bluegill on the line you will want to make sure your drag is set and ready to go.

Fishing Line

The line is THE connection from you to the fish, therefore, it is an important piece of the puzzle and some attention should be paid to its quality, characteristics and condition. It simply amazes me that something so thin has the strength to pull a fighting bluegill from such a distance away. But the line does much more than just pull in fish. It can cause the bait rig to act differently and can give you better or worse feel depending on its characteristics. There are many options when it comes to line choices. The qualities that are most important to a bluegill angler are manageability, lack of visibility to the fish, strength and "feel" qualities. No one line is perfect, but each option has its pros and cons that have to be evaluated.

Monofilament

Monofilament (mono) is a single uniform strand of nylon or polyethylene. It is the most widely used fishing line today because it is the most versatile line on the market while also being a very economical choice. This line will fit most bluegill fishing situations because it has low memory (good manageability) and stretching qualities that are forgiving when bringing in a bigger fish with a light pound test rating. I once brought in a 12 pound catfish on 4 pound test mono using an ultra-light rod. It took nearly 15 minutes of being towed around in the boat before I brought him in and had to remove the last 6 feet of line which had stretched to the point that it appeared to have been melted. But it had held to land fish that was far over the rating of the line. For all of its stretching abilities, it still provides pretty good feel overall.

Many of the top angling professionals still use and rely on this line in many of their fishing situations. It comes in many different formulations to fit different needs, such as: limp, stiff and abrasion resistant. It also is produced in various colors and visibility ranges. It is very good in terms of manageability on a spinning reel and the performance qualities are very good as well. Mono falls somewhere in the mid-range of the visibility scale compared to other lines on the market, but bluegill are rarely line shy to mono. This is due in part to the conditions in which bluegill prefer to live as they are typically in nutrient rich waters that usually have quite a bit of algae and other plant growth. They also tend to bury themselves into tangles of cover where mono will blend in easily to the background.

Mono has a tendency to float which makes jigs fall slower and keep crank baits higher in the water column. This may or may not be a problem depending on the depth you want your bait to be. Usually a slow fall rate is beneficial for bluegill fishing as the bait remains in front of their nose longer tempting them to bite for a longer period of time.

Keep your line fresh by spooling new line at least yearly as exposure to sunlight and the elements will weaken the line over time. Occasionally run your fingers along the last couple feet of your line as you fish. If it feels rough at all, cut that part off and retie your bait. Dragging against objects in the water and the rough mouth parts of fish can cause fray that weakens the line and when you are using a 4 pound test line there isn't much room to move.

There are many manufacturers that produce monofilaments. Premium monofilaments, produced by companies such as Trilene and Stren, are of better quality and more reliable than knock off brands while still being very economical. Premium lines are more uniform throughout the entire length which leads to more consistent performance and is less likely to break.

Copolymer

Copolymerization (copoly) combines two or more nylon or plastics strands into a single line. This structure gives this line more resistance to wear and abrasion. Originally co-poly was much stiffer than mono but changes in the manufacturing process have reduced that problem with some manufacturers being able to make it more manageable. It does have stretch but not as much as mono which gives it a better hook setting quality. Copoly is a more dense line than mono that sinks in the water which can get your bait deeper faster if that is what you need for that presentation, such as a deep running crank bait. The cost is more than mono but generally lower than the alternatives. Because of its construction methods it is thicker in diameter and therefore more visible in the water. It does have some good qualities and should be considered for your outing if it fits your needs for that trip.

Fluorocarbon

Fluorocarbon is made from a polymer of fluorine bonded to carbon. This line has had popularity due to it having almost the same refractive index of water making it virtually invisible in the water. This line does not float due to its density and gets your baits deep quickly. It is also stiffer than mono and while this quality allows you to feel the bottom and any bite better; it causes problems when being wound onto a spinning reel spool and knots sometimes slip out with this line because of its ultra slippery nature. Special knots have been devised and should be used to combat this problem. While this is the line of choice in very clear water, keep in mind that a clear line in green algae filled water will actually stand out.

Most anglers either love or hate this line immediately with very few falling in between because of the stiffness and tendency to twist. It is more expensive than mono by quite a bit but one economical way to use this line when needed is to tie a fluorocarbon leader to your mono backing. Check that connecting knot often, though, to make sure it is not slipping. While I do not recommend this line for every use, it does have a niche to fill if you fish clear water.

Fused and Braided

The last two types of line are fused and braided. These lines are high tech versions of old fashioned thread lines. They are incredibly strong with very narrow diameters but are not transparent like the other lines discussed so they still are more visible in the water. If ripping bait through the water, this is not a problem as the fish will not have time to see the line; however, most of the time we will be fishing slow to moderate speeds which give the bluegill plenty of time to detect the line. It is also a much more expensive line. It simply does not fit for bluegill fishing in most cases.

Properly Filling the Spool on the Reel

Line needs to be filled to the proper level to get the qualities desired from the product. Spin cast and spinning reels should be filled to about 1/8 of an inch below the rim of the spool. If spinning reels are overfilled, line will spool off uncontrollably while under filling results in line drag as it is cast out reducing the distance achieved.

When loading line onto a spinning reel, it is important to feed it on correctly. If the line is fed on incorrectly, it will create an incredible amount of twist that will haunt you every time you fish. The line should come off the new line spool in the same direction that the bail is moving on the reel. Place the spool on the ground and run the line through the guides securing it to the spool. Slowly reel in the new line while keeping slight tension on the line by running it through your fingers or a moist paper towel to reduce heat on your fingers. Keep an eye on the line as it comes into the reel. If a twist develops in the line, turn the spool on the ground over as it is not feeding in correctly. New line on a spinning reel will always have some tendency to twist and come off the spool but following this method will reduce the new line blues.

Bait casting reels are the most forgiving to load new line. Just face the reel right at the spool of new line so that the line is coming straight out to the reel and fill it to within about 1/8th inch of the top of the spool.

To save money and reduce the amount of line being thrown out, only replace the top half of line on the spool. I mentioned before that a spool with too little line on it will affect casting performance and you should never let your line get below half full on the spool. Since we will never go below this level, it makes sense to leave the bottom half on the spool instead of replacing it with new line each time we fill. The old line acts as backing for the new line spliced in on top with a blood knot. This knot is very secure and serves as a reminder to me that I need to add new line if I happen to come to this level during the fishing season. I do replace the backing line every few years to ensure it is strong enough to hold should a fish ever strip out enough line to get into this line.

One last step that helps settle new line on any reel is to stretch it out before fishing. This can be most easily done by dragging a length of line behind a boat going slowly. Feed out enough line without anything tied to it so that the rod is flexed while moving. Continue for a few minutes and then reel in the line while the rod is still flexed. It removes much of the remaining twist and reduces the memory from the line having been held on a larger storage spool in which it was packaged. An alternate method is to allow a stream or river current to take the line and stretch it in the current as you stand stationary. Taking the time to stretch your line prior to fishing will greatly reduce your frustrations with new line.

Fishing Line Summary

Choosing fishing line is very personal since what works for one angler will not necessarily work for the next. The same type of fishing line is also different from one manufacturer to the next. Just because both are labeled 4 pound mono does not mean they are going to act exactly the same. Subtle differences in how they produce their line will result in behavioral differences when you are using it out on the water. Test a few lines by purchasing smaller pony spools and also discuss line usage with other anglers in your area. Local conditions may make one type or brand of line better than the rest. A few quick conversations can lead you in the right direction quicker than blind trial and error over months or years.

Many tackle shops now take old line to recycle it and keep it out of the landfill. Please take advantage of this service where available.

Knots

Care must be taken with knots as while the knot holds the entire rig together it is also inherently the weakest point in the line. Kinks are put in the line by design when a knot is tied but these kinks weaken the line and reduce the amount of stress the line can take before breaking. Also, the friction of the line sliding against line while the knot is being cinched also causes the line to weaken. This friction can be reduced by wetting the line with saliva and taking your time to gently pull alternately on the tag end and main line to tighten it evenly. Saliva is readily available and has properties that make it a better lubricant than water.

Knots for bluegill fishing can be kept fairly simple but there are a few you will want to learn to tie well. The Uni-knot, Clinch knot, Improved Clinch knot, Blood knot and Rapala knot are very good knots to learn for bluegill fishing and are detailed in a step by step fashion on the following pages. If these are not clear enough for you, a quick search of the internet will provide you with live action videos that should make the procedure on how to tie each knot very clear.

This is a very short list of quality knots that I believe will adequately meet your needs when bluegill fishing. There are an infinite number of knots out there that can be used for fishing and you may even eventually choose another for one reason or another. The Palomar knot is an excellent knot to utilize when using the drop shot technique but it will be tied a low percentage of the time and one of the knots here can suffice. This relatively small group is designed to fit your needs while limiting the number of knots that you need to be proficient in tying.

Uni-knot or Duncan's Loop

The uni-knot, or Duncan's loop, is a great all-around knot that can be used to tie on baits, splice one line to another in the case of a leader or attach second bait to the hook bend of the first. It is a durable and strong knot that, once practiced, can be tied in any conditions with ease.

How to tie the Uni-knot

Insert the line into the eye

Pull the line up so a parallel line is formed next to the main line with a long tag end

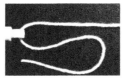

Cross the tag end across the two parallel lines forming a loop on one side

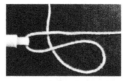

Wrap the tag end around the parallel lines 3-5 times inside the loop that was formed

Wet the line and pull alternately on the main line and tag end until snug then trim the extra line

Clinch and Improved Clinch Knots

The clinch and improved clinch knots are tried and true knots that have been a mainstay for decades. These knots are easy to learn and easy to tie, and many people reply on this knot exclusively. The improved clinch is the slightly better knot of the two since it actually clamps down onto the tag end as it is pulled, preventing slippage.

How to tie the Clinch and Improved Clinch knots

Run the line through the eye of the hook

Twist the line around the main line several times

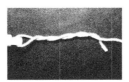

Run the tag end through the small loop created just above the eye of the hook

Wet the line and pull alternately on the main line and tag end until snug then trim the extra line

To tie the improved clinch start with steps 1 through 3 from above and then continue with the next steps

Run the tag end through the new loop that was formed in the last step next to the twisted line

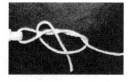

Wet the line and pull alternately on the main line and tag end until snug then trim the extra line

Blood Knot

The blood knot is the most secure knot for splicing two lines together, such as when connecting the backing line of a spool to the new line that will be added on top. Leave very short tag ends when trimming so that it is less likely to slide through. This knot is not near the bait so tag ends really don't affect the fish. Easy to tie in the comfort of your home when you spool up, be sure to wet the line while tightening the knot as there are many wraps that slide over the line until it is secure.

How to tie the Blood knot

Place the two lines parallel to each other with the end in opposite directions

Twist the first line around the second several times

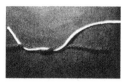

Duck the tag end of the first line between the lines behind the twists created

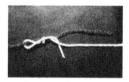

Twist the second line around the first in the opposite rotation as the first

Run the tag end through the loop created between the two twists so that is going through in the opposite direction as the tag end from the first line

Wet the lines and pull alternately on the main lines and tag ends until snug then trim the extra line. Leave just a small tag to prevent slide through

Rapala Knot

The Rapala knot is designed to be tied to crank baits. It leaves a small loop to allow the crank bait to move as designed without restriction. Given that Rapala took the time to design and promote this knot to be used with their infinite array of crank baits, you can be assured it has the desired effect.

How to tie the Rapala knot

Tie an open overhand loop in the line and run the tag end through the eye

Take the tag end through the open loop tied previously

Twist the tag end around the main line several times

Pass the tag end through the original loop again

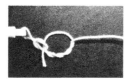

Bring the tag end back up through the new loop formed in the previous step

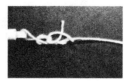

Wet the lines and pull alternately on the main lines and tag ends until snug then trim the extra line

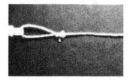

Basic Terminal Tackle

Terminal tackle for bluegill is luckily fairly straightforward and uncomplicated. Since bluegills target smaller prey items, we have to keep our presentations relatively small and light. Big oversized baits or excessive tackle on the line will result in undue weight and cause the presentation to appear unnatural. Bluegills spend their lives inspecting small organisms they prey on and will pick up on any unnatural movements or appearances. It is up to us to give them an offering with as little extra hardware as possible.

Hooks

Hooks should be fairly small to fit into the bluegill's mouth but not so small that they completely swallow it and get gut hooked. The best hook sizes to use for bluegill are in the size range of 6 through 10. Hook sizes get smaller as the number increases when using whole numbers, so a 6 is much larger than a 10. Using hooks on the larger end of this range will serve to select out to catch only the large bluegill in the population since the small ones won't be able to get their mouths around the hook bend. However, if you prefer to catch more numbers of fish a smaller hook will allow more of the school to be caught.

Most bluegill anglers prefer thin wired hooks as they pierce the mouth easier than thicker hooks and are also easier to remove. Thinner wired hooks will also bend if they become snagged which allows you to still retrieve your bait and tackle. The hook can then be quickly bent back into shape once it is retrieved.

Hooks can be modified to make them easier to remove by smashing down the barb of the hook. If you choose to mash down the barb, make sure to keep the line tight while reeling in the bluegill because it will also make it easier for the fish to throw the hook.

The preferred hook for bluegill is the classic Aberdeen which is a long shank hook for live bait purposes. It is easy for the bluegill to pull into their mouth, holds bait well and the long shank provides good leverage to remove the hook. A few other classic live bait hooks that come in bluegill appropriate sizes are the wide gap bait holder, salmon egg, octopus and long shank. All of these come in various eye configurations that will hold the bait in differing positions in the water.

Circle hooks are a relatively new addition to the freshwater ranks. At this time they are not currently produced in sizes below a 6. When using these hooks, you cannot set the hook like you would with any other hook. Patience is a must when using these hooks as slight pressure on the line as the fish swims away will cause the hook to set in the corner of the fish's mouth. Many anglers who use this hook for other species claim higher hook up percentages. It is better with live baits as the fish needs to hold the bait in its mouth for an extended period to set the hook.

Hooks can be paired with about anything when it comes to bluegill fishing. Soft plastics, live bait and prepared baits can be offered to them with very little weight for them to detect. I recommend that you start with the classic style Aberdeen hooks. They are classic for a reason, they work. As with everything else, be willing to experiment and have a selection ready to go. Different eye configurations and shank lengths will vary the action of your bait slightly which may trigger the bite that day, so keeping a few different hooks in the tackle box is always a good idea.

Jigs

Jigs are an incredibly versatile piece of terminal tackle. A simple hunk of lead molded around the eye of the hook, a jig is a hook and weight all in one that can be tipped with thousands of baits. The weight of the jig increases the casting distance of the offering and keeps it in place better in current and wind. There are hundreds if not thousands of options to pair with a jig such as various types of live baits, soft plastics and prepared baits. Jigs come in differing shapes and sizes that will fall through the water column at different rates. A slow rate of decent keeps the bait in front of a fish longer making it a more enticing meal for them to pursue. Sizes most common when using spinning gear are $1/64^{th}$, $1/32^{nd}$, $1/16^{th}$ and $1/8^{th}$ ounces. The various jig weights are paired with correspondingly sized hooks that are appropriate for bluegill fishing. Wind and current will play a factor

 in which size you will be able to use on a given day. Wind will stop a cast before it reaches the target area if the size is too small and strong wind will even push the line hanging above the surface of the water which pulls the bait to the surface.

Northland is famous for producing the classic gumball shaped jig which is more or less a ball at the front end with a collar to hold the bait onto the shank. These work great for holding most plastics but the thickness of the collar can split small soft plastics that are good to use for bluegill. One option is to mash down the collar with pliers. The other option is to switch to jigs produced for live bait or fly fishing as they lack this collar. A dab of superglue will keep the soft plastic from sliding down the shank should this become an issue.

A few jigs have spinners molded into the head of the jig to give a flash as they are brought through the water. Blakemore Roadrunner was one of the first to do this and is so successful that others have jumped into this category with a version of their own. The flash from the tiny spinner draws the attention of many predators as it resembles the silvery flash from the side of a fry or small minnow. And the placement of this spinner so close to the bait gets them zeroed in on the offering. When the sun is out, this can be a deadly jig to use.

Some jigs now come with bodies already loaded onto the shank and ready to go. The body is matched to a formed head that gives the jig a complete visual package and are jig versions of crank baits. The advantage these jigs have over crank baits though is that they can be fished in a wide variety of methods and at different depths whereas most crank baits have a limited depth range and speed of retrieval to impart the proper action of the bait.

Ice fishing jigs are productive all year round, so don't put them away when the ice melts. These tiny jigs can be used alone or tied on as trailers to larger baits to give the bluegill an easy target. Tipped with live bait like wax worms or prepared baits they are usually too good to pass up for a bluegill.

Jigs come in an endless array of colors: solid, multi-colored, glowing, textured, and on and on. Color can be used to draw attention with a bit of flash or to look natural and unassuming. Bright colors are typically best in clear and bright conditions such as white, chartreuse, yellows and oranges. In low light conditions or stained/murky water, darker colors stand out better from the background. Colors such as black, brown and olive are good selections for murky water. The majority of the time, our quarry will be in shallow clear water with good light. Therefore we stock more of the brighter colored jigs but should always have a few of the darker colored jigs available for the murky adverse conditions.

Needless to say, jigs are an important tool to have in your tackle box. They are incredibly versatile and having a good selection of colors, sizes and shapes will have you prepared for any situation.

Bobbers

Bobbers, or floats, are the iconic image most defer to when they think of bluegill fishing with a little boy with a cane pole sitting on the shore with a bobber floating in the water. While this is a nostalgic image, the fact is that a bobber can be a very useful and effective tool to use when bluegill fishing. It can be used to get the bait to a location, keep it in the strike zone infinitely longer and finally detect the bite. While the classic ball shaped bobber is still the dominant shape that most gravitate towards, there is an infinite array of shapes, sizes and special features to consider. Each type of bobber has a specific function that will help you catch bluegill if used correctly.

Ball and teardrop shaped bobbers are good general use selections. They make a splash when landing that can serve to attract actively feeding bluegill but can spook inactive fish. The line can be quickly attached with either the top or bottom clip but is more secure when passed through both. Teardrops can either be attached with the point towards the bait or towards the rod. If it is positioned towards the bait, the idea is that it will sink into the water with less resistance and the fish won't feel it as much. Rigged with the point towards the rod helps the bobber to track straight through the water as it is reeled in while swimming the bait slowly back to you. Both the round and teardrop bobbers are excellent general purpose tackle.

Pencil style bobbers are great when the fish are less active and skittish. They have less of a splashdown and their ultra-thin profile leads to very little resistance when the fish pulls them down into the water. Unique to pencil bobbers is the ability to detect the up bite when rigged properly. An up bite is when the bluegill takes the bait while moving up in the water column. Any other bobber will only raise an imperceptible amount in the water while the line under goes slack and the bluegill makes off with your bait. When weighted correctly the pencil bobber will ride in the water at a 45 degree angle. When a fish takes it with an up bite, the bobber will lay over on the surface indicating slack line below. Any other bobber will only rise so slightly, if at all, in the water that you will never know what is happening until it is too late and the bluegill is gut hooked or, more likely, strips your bait and swims away. The weight ratio of the bait rig will have to be matched with the bobber to achieve the 45 degree angle which can be accomplished with changing the size of the bait or bobber. One or two of these in your tackle box is enough to have on hand when the bites are subtle.

Cigar bobbers are the pencil bobber's chubby cousin. They generally perform the same but are larger and less dynamic than their thinner counterparts. It is nearly impossible to adjust these to detect an up bite but they do indicate bites with much action and wobble.

Slip bobbers are designed for fishing a little deeper. Usually once the bobber is set at more than a five foot depth, casting becomes a nightmare. The weight of the bait and the bobber causes the line to twist and snag on itself when you cast out. A slip bobber slides on the line so that it is riding on the bait at the cast and moves up to a bobber stop once it hits the water and the bait sinks. The disadvantage to this system is that the hook has to be removed, bobber stop placed on the line at the depth desired, line run through the bobber and the bait tied back on before fishing again. It takes some time when you consider that in three seconds, a standard bobber can be clipped on or off the line and fishing continues. Most of the time, bluegill are in the shallower depths and typically do not require a deep presentation making this bobber less often used.

Popper bobbers are another specialty bobber. It has a teardrop bottom and a concave top. When pulled or jerked it pops and splashes the waters surface like a wounded minnow or insect similar with a similar commotion to some top water baits designed for bass. When fish are actively feeding, this splashing is a dinner bell that brings them quickly into the area and sends them into a feeding frenzy. While effective at producing this action, a round bobber can be jerked to accomplish almost the same action and is more versatile.

Weighted bobbers and adjust-a-bubbles are great for casting out flies, light weighted baits and casting against a wind. The casting bubble, or adjust-a-bubbles, is a line through bobber much like a slip bobber with an elongated tear drop shape. Weight is added to the bobber by separating the halves and allowing water to enter and then secured to the line by twisting the two halves in opposite directions. The  water inside acts as casting weight while in the air but the air inside keeps it buoyant. The water inside has neutral buoyancy so the amount of air inside can be adjusted so that the bobber barely floats when the bait is down. This gives it incredibly little resistance when the bluegill pulls it under. Weighted bobbers have a lead collar next to the clip on the bottom end. While it casts far, it is not as versatile as the casting bubble as it cannot be adjusted to match the weight of the bait. These are good bobbers to have in case it gets windy next time you are out on the water.

Bobbers are a must for the bluegill angler. They can be indispensable and add a whole new dimension to the action that you can impart on your bait rig. They can hold bait perfectly still, swim bait in at a very controlled depth and used as a bluegill attractor itself. Having a selection of sizes and shapes will increase your odds of having the right one for the conditions that day.

Basic Tackle Wrap-up

With a collection of this basic terminal, an angler is able to catch large numbers of bluegill in any body of water. More terminal tackle will be discussed in the following sections, but this tackle is merely complex versions of hooks and jigs with attractants added to them. There is something to be said to keeping things simple and fun and basic tackle was used for hundreds of years very successfully. However, adding the following options to your arsenal will make you a more productive and effective bluegill angler.

Live Bait

Live bait has long been the gold standard for catching bluegills. It was the original bait and for thousands of years as there was simply no other choice. Run a hook through a small critter; add a little weight to cast out and you are in business. The familiarity of the bait to the bluegill as a food item combined with natural action and that delicious natural taste is just too much for them to resist. Mounted on a hook or jig they can be bounced on the bottom or suspended near the surface to match the bluegill's depth.

Crickets are outstanding live bait for big bluegills. Bluegills often search out terrestrial insects that get blown into the pond from the surrounding grasses and a cricket is a common fat bodied morsel they are used to targeting. The kicking legs are a dinner bell that the bluegill will come rushing in to investigate. Crickets are sometimes a challenge to find in bait shops but can be found in some pet stores, under most logs and in many garages (especially late at night when the angler is trying to sleep the night before heading out to fish).

Worms (night crawlers and garden worms) are another good live bait option. They are readily available in bait shops, vend-a-baits and at many gas stations and bluegill are familiar with them as a food item. Fat night crawlers, or chunks of them, are tasty bits the bluegill can't resist. Don't load on too much or the tricky gill will strip off all

85

of the free parts and fill up before getting hooked as the tissue of the night crawler is soft and easily pulled from the shank of the hook. The red wiggler, or garden worm, has a little different body type. The body of this worm is less bulky and a little tougher. By hooking the body several times it leaves enough to wiggle and keeps it close to the hook point while the folds make it appear fatter and juicier. Your chances of hooking up with a garden worm are better given these traits and how you can rig this worm. Keep your worms cool by placing them in the shade or even on ice. A fresh worm is much livelier and attracts a bite much better than a limp lifeless offering.

Wax worms are the staple in the winter for ice fishing but can be great bait any time of year. They are just as easily found in bait shops and gas stations on the way to the water as worms. They are small bite sized morsels a bluegill will recognize and a pinched wax worm emits a scent that is to bluegill as chum is to a shark. A smashed wax worm held vertically in place by a bobber creates a scent cloud around the bait that the bluegills can zone in on to attack. Don't be shy with wax worms as more are better when baiting up. A group of 2 or 3 wax worms on the hook gives the bait a larger profile and is more attractive to a bluegill drawing the bite quicker. While the middle of the worm is mush, the outer skin is tough enough to endure a few nibbles before they fall off, giving you time to set the hook.

When the bite is tough, nothing beats live bait. Some argue that live bait is the best in any situation, but I respectfully disagree. The downside to live bait is getting fresh bait, keeping it alive and in an active condition while out on the pond. Live bait also needs to be replaced often since it can be pulled off the hook relatively easily and it looses its vigor as it soaks in the water. This should be one tool in your tackle box; not the only tool.

Artificial Baits

The first artificial baits were hand tied flies made for hundreds of years with fur, hair and other naturally occurring materials to resemble preferred prey items of fish. But now we no longer have to create our own as technology has progressed and there are a multitude of artificial baits manufactured with lifelike appearance and action. Artificial baits are ready to go at a moments notice without having to stop by the bait shop before heading out to fish with all the appearance, action and even scent of natural baits. These baits are more durable and can be used for long periods of time without having to be replaced like live baits require.

Color Selection

Artificial baits come in an infinite array of colors and it can be overwhelming trying to select the perfect one for each situation so keep it as simple as possible. The obvious goal is to get the bait noticed to trigger a bite. A good rule of thumb is that brighter colors are better to use in clear water and sunny conditions, while dark colors are better in murky water and cloudy conditions. Four good colors to have on hand are white, chartreuse, pumpkin seed and black. These four simple colors cover most situations encountered and make it easy to make quick decisions when on the water. Other colors can, and should, be added to your arsenal over time but these four can help you make faster decisions and act on them.

Soft Plastics

Soft plastics come in thousands of shapes, sizes and colors. Some exactly match a specific prey item, such as a cricket or minnow, while others, such as a tube, have a shape that can be made to look like a variety of bluegill prey depending on how it is retrieved. The action of modern soft plastics is amazing and far from the stiff rubber baits that were produced just a few years ago. Now it is possible to give lifelike action to even the smallest of baits with free moving appendages and tails that emulate fins and legs wiggling in the water.

The tube has a general appearance that looks like nothing yet just about anything all at the same time with the angler imparting most of the action to the bait. Tubes come in both solid and hollow bodies which affects the profile size. The hollow tube has a slim profile while a solid body tube has a fatter body and the skirt is sometimes flared out making it a much larger profile by comparison. The skirt of the tube moves in the water to appear like the shimmering sides of a fry or the legs of a small insect. Modifying the skirt by removing roughly every other tentacle of the skirt will give it more action by allowing space for it to move. Sometimes this extra action is just the trigger that gets the bluegill to bite. Tubes can be rigged onto jig heads, plain hooks or specialty jig heads designed to be inserted into the tube for endless action possibilities. A steady retrieve gives the appearance of a minnow cruising through the water while dragging the tube slowly across the bottom imparts more of a crayfish or insect impression. Jigging the rod an inch or two while steadily retrieving the bait makes the tube jump and dart like a frightened fry or insect. This is a very versatile bait that once mastered can be used in every situation. Stock many styles and colors of this bait and be ready to use them.

Grubs have a short solid body that is cylindrical in shape with ridges or bumps that run along the length of the body much like a wax worm. Originally it was very plain bait with only two short stubs that extended out of the back of the body past the bend of the hook. All action of this bait was dependent on the angler in how they retrieved the bait. That was when technology had not been able to impart the action of the soft plastics to smaller baits and it was fairly hard and rigid. It was the preferred bait to use in conjunction with the safety pin style spinner bait aptly named a beetle spin. This soft plastic can still be found on the market today but is dwarfed by its descendants such as the curly tailed grub.

Twister tails, or curly tailed grubs, have a grub body with a flat C-shaped curled tail trailing behind. The tail imparts a twisting corkscrew action while being retrieved that gives the bait incredible action. When the bait is paused the tail will cease its corkscrew motion and curl back into its original shape and slowly sway in any current. This almost constant action makes it much less dependent on the angler for action. This bait is usually retrieved in a steady cadence with some level of jigging to impart the action of an injured fry, tadpole or insect swimming through the water column. Popping the twister with a short jigging action will replicate an escape attempt and many times this action will trigger the bluegill to bite. Color choices are again endless with solid, two color and tri-color options. Sometimes the flash or a bright tail will get the bluegill interested while at other times more muted tail color gives a more natural appearance. Twin tailed twisters have two tails curving towards each other and when swimming, it gives the profile of a small frog or multi-legged insect. Twister tails are an excellent soft plastic that has great action and many retrieval possibilities.

Slider grubs are a grub body with a flat club-like tail attached to the main body by a thin strip of plastic. This thin tail allows the club tail a lot of freedom to move and wiggle while the bait is swam through the water. It gives a very good minnow or fry simulation as it slides through the water. This is great bait for covering water searching for bluegills or slow trolling.

Beaver tail grubs have a flat wide tail attached to the grub body. The wide tail is usually a little wider than the body and thick enough to be somewhat rigid. It is another generalist bait that really doesn't look exactly like a specific prey but has a good action the bluegill seem to really like. The tail causes the grub to glide and dart as it is swam and jigged giving it an excellent erratic action. This soft bait can emulate fry, small crustacean or insect but the angler will have to impart much of the action since the tail is fairly rigid.

True minnow imitations are molded to look exactly like a minnow's body in profile. They are thick across the top with a narrower belly and a club tail, similar to the slider, for a wiggle action when retrieved. These are good but are very specific and only work if bluegills are targeting minnows or fry at that specific time.

Small soft plastic worms come in a variety of shapes and sizes. Some are fat little wax worm imitations while other are more like a thin garden worm. Action varies greatly depending on the thickness and type of material used to produce the worm. Each will need to be evaluated on its own merits before being put into use. Bluegills can't resist a juicy worm when it is placed in front of them, and if you don't have any live worms at hand these will fit the need.

As technology has gotten better for soft plastics, exact replicas of insects have hit the market. Crickets, nymphs, hellgrammites and more now come bagged up and ready to go. Action will vary between manufactures as body styles and plastic composition will vary. Select baits with a very soft composition with free moving legs and appendages for the most action possible. Squirmy little bugs are a huge energy source for a bluegill and they will pursue this prey item with vigor. These are excellent baits to have on supply in the tackle box.

Soft plastics are an absolute must have for any serious bluegill angler. They are always ready to go and fit many situations encountered. The only down side to a soft plastic bait is that they do not taste like live bait to a bluegill and can be quickly spit back out before the hook is set. But we have technology on our side again as many soft plastics come impregnated with a variety of scents that the bluegill finds very desirable. Any soft plastic without this feature can be enhanced by simply tipping the hook with prepared bait which will be discussed shortly. These scents turn inactive bluegills into active fish and keep them holding onto the bait just a bit longer so you have time to set the hook. Soft plastics are great on their on and once combined with a scent they become fish magnets.

Spinner Baits

Spinner baits impart both flash and vibrations which grab the attention of active bluegills from a distance. This bait moves rather quickly so the fish need to be actively feeding to pursue this presentation as it will not be in the strike zone for very long. On a clear day the spinner grabs the sunlight and reflects it out into the water simulating the flash of a minnow's side. The blades come in many colors and sizes with silver and gold being the most common. Silver is better for clear water with bright flashes while gold is better for murky conditions. Common blade shapes are Colorado and willow leaf. The wider Colorado blade rotates slower and gives off more vibrations combined with larger flashes of reflected light. The narrow willow leaf blade rotates faster with less vibration but sends out more flashes more rapidly.

The in-line spinner has been in use for decades and is comprised of a straight wire shaft with a blade in the front, a solid weight for a body on the wire, and a treble hook connected at the rear. The treble hook is sometimes adorned with tufts of various colored hair to add a little attention getter while concealing the hook. It is excellent on active bluegill. Just cast them out and reel it back while the bait does all the work flashing and thumping its blade as it goes through the water. This bait does have a tendency to rotate because of the design and can put a twist into the line. A good way to prevent this is to tie a swivel about a foot above the spinner which allows the rotation while keeping your line twist free.

The safety-pin style spinning bait has a blade offset from the bait, usually a soft plastic, with an angled wire. The Johnson Beetle Spin was the original to bring this style of bait to the small size we use

 and is still very effective. With a small silver Colorado blade and plastic grub bait on the other side, it is simple and effective. You can bring it in fast for a fleeing prey presentation, slow roll for

less active fish or even jig it and allow it to fall which imparts a dying prey action. Other small safety-pin style spinner baits have been developed over the years but it's hard to beat the beetle spin. The bait side even has a clasp that can be opened to quickly swap out jigs or other baits to fine tune the presentation.

Don't forget the most compact spinner on the market that was discussed earlier in the jig section. The RoadRunner falls into both categories with the spinner mounted right onto the head of the jig to get the flash right next to the bait. Fish them fast or slow like you would normally fish a jig and the blade adds a whole new wrinkle to your presentation. The quick  flash of the spinner beating against the side of the bait as you swim it in rapidly or the lazy flash of the spinner as the jig is being slowly bounced across the bottom catches the bluegill's eye and gets them interested.

Spinners are a good thing to have on hand when the fish are active and the sun is shining. Fish them both on the surface and down a few feet as they will still reflect light at this depth and give off vibrations. They can provide some exciting fish action.

Crank Baits

I know, "Crank baits for bluegill?" Absolutely! There are many great micro sized crank baits out there that have amazing action and will bring in big bluegill. Good bluegill size cranks are in the 1-1 ½ inch range. Shallow diving crank baits can be run next to shore and over top of submerged structure drawing the bluegill up to feed. No need for a special rod for these as their light weight and tight wobbles

are easily handled by a light power fast action setup. Vary the retrieve and pause it at times as these atypical actions in the middle of a retrieve will often elicit a bite. You don't need hundreds of these micro crank baits but few options should be enough. While smaller bluegill will investigate and even peck at this bait, only the bigger bluegills are aggressive and large enough to attack these larger baits. If your goal is big bluegill, this is an option you must use.

Flies

Flies can be either purchased or tied at home. While the object is to make the fly appear and act as natural as possible when fishing, don't get too caught up in that. Many a meticulous fly has been tied more for the sake of the angler than the bluegill. Bluegills like swimming actions and dangling legs that look mostly like swimming fish fry and insects. With that in mind, concentrate on having a supply of streamers, floating insects, submerged insects and poppers when tying and selecting flies to use. Retailers carry styles of all of these fly types and they are simple to tie yourself. I tie a number of each during the slow winter months that keep me supplied throughout the entire fishing season, and to prevent me from going insane waiting for open water. Focus more on the action and function of the fly rather than the aesthetics. I have detailed a few of my favorites below that I keep ready to go.

Streamers are designed to appear as small fish fry or minnows that are streaking through the water trying to find a safe place to hide. A simple fly to tie with a bead for the head and a marabou tail will give that action.

Simple Streamer

Run a bead onto a #10 or #12 hook. Wrap the shank with thread and secure the bead into place.

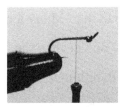

Tie in a length of marabou roughly the length of the shank of the hook.

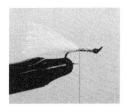

Tie in chenille at the rear of the fly and run the thread forward to the eye. Wrap the chenille forward and secure with thread. Finish with a double whip finish.

Floating insects are deadly in the summer when terrestrial bugs are at their height and are often blown into the water. Use a fly with many legs that dangle in the water and move freely when retrieved. Bluegills don't typically gently suck the fly in like a trout. They are more of a beer drinker's fish and they slurp the insect in with a very audible and distinctive sound that is often the first sign you have a bite even before you feel the weight of the fish. Foam flies are easy to tie and very durable. One of my favorites is the foam spider with a small body and long legs made of rubber hackle that has wild action.

Foam Spider

Wrap the shank of a #10 or #12 hook with thread and secure a piece of foam or pre-shaped foam spider body to the far end.

Wrap the thread forward and tie in two lengths of 2" long pieces of rubber hackle onto each side of the hook shank.

Wrap the thread forward and secure the front of the foam spider body top the shank.

Finish with a double whip finish and trim legs to length if needed.

Submerged insects are good most of the year as bluegill will always jump the chance to eat a juicy water bug. Again, active legs on the fly really draw in the bite. Rubber hackle and a simple body form are the rule again with this fly. But instead of a foam body, one of chenille with a couple wraps of lead wire will make the fly fall slowly through the water column keeping it in front of the bluegill longer. Offsetting the lead wrap towards one end or the other makes the fall more erratic giving a wounded creature appearance.

Bluegill Bug

Wrap the shank of a #10 or #12 hook with thread. Wrap 3 to 5 turns of lead onto the shank off center towards the bend and tie in with thread.

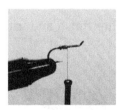

Tie in chenille and move the thread forward to just in front of the lead. Tie in two pieces of 2" long rubber hackle so that it sticks out at 90 degree angles from the body of the fly.

Wrap the chenille forward being careful to allow the rubber hackle to remain sticking out at 90 degree angles.

Finish with a double whip finish.

The popper has been in the retail shop forever and is still readily available. Pulled across the surface of the water in short bursts, the curve in the nose of the bait pops and splashes the water in front of it disturbing the surface. This action brings in the active fish to inspect and attack the wounded prey item. I also tie a popper of my own that works great on its own or with a streamer trailer tied to the hook bend.

Foam Popper

Wrap the shank of a #8 or #10 hook with thread.

Attach a tail of rubber hackle or marabou roughly the same length as the shank of the hook.

Trim a length of cylinder foam to the length of the shank of the hook and poke a hole with a small pin. Slide the foam onto the shank and secure with the thread making a figure eight connecting the front to back under the foam and complete with a double whip finish.

Ice Fishing Jigs

These tiny jigs can and should be used year round. While they are the best option during the hard water seasons, they are small and attractive enough to use any time. Most have the weight of the jig molded into the body shape of the bait making them compact and an easy meal for a bluegill. Some also have tiny spinner blades that catch light and flash to draw attention to them. Tipping them with wax worms or prepared baits add to their attractiveness. Used alone or trailed behind larger bait rigs they can draw a bite when other presentations are failing, especially when the weather is changing.

Prepared Baits

Prepared baits are concoctions either made at home or commercially that are designed to smell like a real food item the bluegill would normally consume. In the fish world, smell is a much more important sense than taste to let the fish know if the object is a food item that should be consumed and is very a powerful trigger. Like humans, scent plays a large role in the taste of the food item and will get the bluegill to hold onto the bait a bit longer. Adding these to plastic baits makes them more effective and increases the number of bluegills caught. Usually in the form of a paste or dough, some prepared baits have been fashioned into various shapes or infused into soft plastics to increase their appeal to the fish by also appearing like prey.

Homemade prepared baits can be made inexpensively at home with simple ingredients found around the house. There are hundreds if not thousands of recipes and each "cook" usually likes to put their own variation on each to make it their own. Some are as simple as bread and water to produce a doughy substance that can be colored with food coloring and added to the hook. Others involve a more complex mixture with flour and water as the base and a wide array of ingredients from the kitchen or purchased online for scent. While these concoctions are less expensive, most are not as durable as commercial prepared baits. Also, the professionals have the advantage of being able to utilize amino acids which comprise much of the odors in nature making them much more realistic and appealing to the bluegill. Much like tying your own flies, making your own prepared baits can be fun and rewarding when you entice a fish to bite something you created, but commercial baits tend to be more effective and durable.

Prepared dough baits are readily available commercially. The catfish anglers were the first to really make this type of bait popular, but it has slowly spread to other species including bluegills. Dough baits can be quickly added to any bait rig for a little added attractant to get interest and trigger the bite. These baits get soft when wet and do not stand up well to being repeatedly cast out, but if you fish this bait properly you can turn the soft nature into an asset. When vertical fished or held under a bobber, the prepared bait will slowly emit a cloud around the bait creating a chum-like effect that will get the bluegill motivated to bite. It can be a complete game changer when the fish are inactive and the bite is off. I highly recommend having a jar of this with you at all times when fishing.

Formed prepared baits are the gold standard of prepared baits as they have the shape, action and scent of live bait. Many companies have products in this category with many body styles, actions and scents. From large insect, minnow and worm imitations to corn and grubs that are small enough to be used as bait or tip other baits the options available increase every year and the formulations improve constantly. Some are simply plastic baits with the scent infused while other are made entirely from a biodegradable compounds that emits scent constantly while in the water. This category is advancing so rapidly it is impossible to cover all of the options available to the angler as tomorrow there will be more. I absolutely recommend having these baits in your arsenal. They come in about any shape you could want and fish better than live bait. It is durable enough to stay on the hook through an entire day of fishing and the scents truly fool the fish into thinking it is live prey.

Prepared bait is vital to have on any bluegill expedition. They outperform live bait by being more durable, easier to use and store infinitely longer than anything alive. When added to any other artificial they make that bait perform exponentially better. I simply don't go bluegill fishing without some sort of prepared bait.

Electronics

Electronic devices are not compulsory for bluegill fishing but can be a very useful tool to use. Electronics mark locations to return to in the future, indicate depth accurately and mark underwater structures that may otherwise never be found. You will learn new waters faster and learn new things about your regular fishing locations that will surprise you.

GPS units are very portable and flexible. A simple hand held unit can be used to mark locations where you were successful in catching bluegill so you are able to return later without tipping off other anglers to your favored location. Depending on the unit, notes and information can be entered right into the unit to remind you how your success was achieved the last time you were there. Otherwise a notebook combined with a few waypoints will serve to remind you quickly what is happening at that location. Information such as date, time of day and bait used will get you catching fish faster without you having to remember the details from the previous trip. And when that trip was months or years ago, this information can be incredibly helpful.

Fish finders, or sonars, can alert you to fish swimming below your boat but they do much more than that. They give you a detailed picture of the bottom depths and structures that hold fish at different times of the year. In new waters, you can locate structures to fish so you are productive more rapidly. In water you fish often, it will reveal structures and features you may have been passing over. If the sonar unit you are using has a function that shows fish with little fish images, turn it off. By using this mode, you will miss an incredible amount of detail as it tries to "clean" the image for you. Take the time to learn to use the sonar and interpret the images displayed to decipher bottom compositions, structures and fish detected. At first it seems daunting but it will come to you quickly. And don't rely on the sample images supplied in the manual or in demo mode because the unit will almost never display a perfect display such that they show. Given the various units on the market and the features each has, I recommend going onto the Internet to watch a video specific to your make and model for a quick tutorial that shows real world conditions. A short video can show you how to set your unit up and how to read the image very well.

Cameras leave no doubt as to what is happening under the surface. You will see right on the screen what is happening directly below you at that moment. The limitations of the camera are that it is time consuming to operate and you only see a limited distance. The danger is that an angler spends more time watching their screen instead of catching the fish. Also, the cost to reward ratio of this piece of equipment is pretty high. It is definitely not for everyone, but you may find it useful.

Electronics can be an angler's friend if used properly. They are tools that are part of the process, not the entire process, so try not to fixate on them. Use them for what they are designed for, which is to help you formulate a plan of attack and confirm or deny your suspicions of what the fish are doing and where they are located. Portable electronics allow you to be mobile and use various method of fishing. I use a basic portable sonar unit coupled with a handheld GPS to make me more effective at catching bluegill while staying light, flexible and highly mobile.

Maps

A topographical map is a very useful tool both before heading out to fish and while out on the water. Studying a map before even setting eyes on the water allows the angler to understand what that lake has to offer in the way of depths, points, protected bays/coves, channels and more. Taking this information combined with variables such as: season, recent weather, preferred depths for those conditions and habitat available, will give us a complete picture of what is most likely happening with the bluegill and where there is a good chance they will be located. Armed with this knowledge of the lake and a good game plan, we can target good locations first which increases our chances of quick success. We also will have a better idea of the bait rig and techniques to use to draw out the bite in those locations. Should the preplanned tactics prove to be incorrect or the bite is slow to come, a quick check of the map will help us quickly devise an alternative plan while still on the water.

Not all bodies of water will have a complete topographical map but larger lakes usually do. These maps often include extraneous information such as seasonal hot spots and other structures such as stumps, weed beds and old road beds. Using all of this information plus what you know about bluegills will increase your odds of catching big bluegills. Paper maps laminated to prevent water damage were once the most advanced but now maps can be downloaded to your computer, sonar or GPS. These maps can be marked with locations you want to investigate and locations that proved to be successful with a few notes added for quick reference next time you head out fishing.

Smaller lakes and ponds may not have these detailed topographical maps, but often a local bait shop, Lake Manager or other local resident will have drawn a relatively crude map. Do not scoff at these less technical maps as they still can hold very valuable information. General depths and possible structures to focus our efforts can be found. Just keep in mind that these maps are not to scale and never dead-on accurate so finding specific structures may take a little searching.

Combining the knowledge we have on the bluegill's habits and habitat with a map containing as much detailed information as possible can give us an edge to finding bluegill quickly and being more productive on any given day. A plan can be created to make best use of the time we have to go fishing and make the outing more fun and successful. As the bluegills tell us how well we planned, adjustments can be made to hone in on their location and use a presentation that works. While not crucial, maps are a bonus that should be used when possible.

Section 3:

Putting Our Tackle to Work

We know about the fish in terms of where it lives, what it eats, seasonal movements, preferred habitat and tackle that can help us catch them. It is time to get serious and focus on how to put this knowledge to use and catch the big bluegills. Giant slabs are a blast to catch and will put up a tremendous fight against the light tackle we use during our expeditions.

Techniques to Catching Big Bluegill

Baits need to be presented to the bluegill in a manner that entices them to take action and bite. The presentation is a combination of action or inactivity designed to give the bait the appearance of a natural prey item that the bluegill will find appealing enough to bite at that given time of year and day. This section illustrates many techniques that are very effective in catching bluegill consistently.

Bobber Fishing

Bobber fishing is the iconic image of fishing for bluegill and for good reason. It works! A bobber holds the bait at a very specific level where a bluegill can inspect and take the offering while not being hurried. Bluegills generally feed on prey that is above them, except for Redear which feed on snails found on the bottom. A bobber holds a bait rig just above the bluegill, tempting them to come up and investigate. It is quick and easy to adjust the depth level of the bait until success is accomplished and then returned to that exact depth and location once one bluegill is caught. Generally speaking, once you find an active fish at a certain level in the water column, others will also be active at or near that same depth throughout that body of water. Bobbers can get you to that level easily and consistently.

Most believe that the bait under the bobber is being held dead still but this is rarely the case. Only if the water's surface is totally calm will the bait be completely still. Most of the time there is some type of wind or breeze creating waves or small ripples that gently bounce the bobber on the surface. This action is transferred to the bait below giving it an animated life-like appearance with small erratic movements.

There is a myth that the angler should cast the bobber rig out and not move it at all until a bite is detected. This is completely wrong. While there are times when the bluegills prefer bait with little action, other times action of some type will be required to trigger the bite. Many different actions can be imparted to the bait with a bobber that cannot be achieved any other way. Some are reeling steadily, jerking the bobber, or reeling with pauses which raises the bait in the water column and then swings it down to the maximum depth when paused. These techniques give the bait great action while retaining an exact depth which is almost impossible with any other technique.

Bobbers are more than simple strike indicators. They are depth control devices that should be used to their fullest potential to get the bait right in front of the bluegill and hold it there to entice the bite. Having a range of sizes and shapes in your tackle box is a very good idea so you have the one that fits your needs in any situation you may encounter.

Jigging

Jigging is the term generally used to describe moving bait through the water with small hops and jerks. It is typically done using a jig head as terminal tackle but can be imparted to just about any hook, crank bait, spinner bait or other weighted rig. The action is accomplished with various sized movements of the end of your rod while reeling in the bait, dragging it across the bottom, vertical fishing directly below you, or trolling it behind the boat. The speed and ferocity of the bait's movements is determined by the distance the rod tip is moved and the force you impart combined and the weight and shape of your bait. A two to four inch rod tip movement of a certain pressure will move a jig that is 1/32oz further than a 1/4oz jig. The jerk will pull the bait up and forward at which point it will fall until the line is tight again with most fish will strike the bait during this fall. Slowly and constantly reeling in during the jerk and pause process keeps the line tight and you in contact with the bait so you can feel when a bluegill takes the bait.

The angler is in control of the distance the bait moves with each jig and the cadence of those movements. Both of these factors are very important to triggering the bite. A slow less violent jig action with a slow cadence is required for less actively feeding bluegills while a more violent jerk in a more rapid cadence will get active bluegill chasing down the bait.

Jigging is a fairly simple technique to learn and will give you infinite possibilities on your retrievals. It can be performed near structure, on the bottom, in open water or any other place you can cast your rig. The jerk and pause motion is a natural motion for prey items in nature which gets the attention of bluegill and brings them in close to take the offering. Much like shaking a string in front of a playful cat, bluegills find this action hard to resist.

Swimming a Bait

Swimming bait is a simple retrieve that will work to catch bluegills while covering an area rather quickly. Just reel the bait rig back in at a steady speed. The speed of retrieval can be quickly changed until the correct speed is found to match the mood of the bluegill that day. Your bait will glide through the water like a small creature swimming to cover. When brought near a large bluegill, it appears to be an easy meal that will require little effort to capture and they tend to slash at it quickly before it swims out of range. Of course, the fish will have to be at least moderately active or they may just watch it swim by unless you almost bump it off their nose. The swimming action can be imparted to just about any bait rig with success.

Vertical Fishing

Vertical fishing is concentrating on a column of water and working it from top to bottom. This can be done from a boat, on the ice, off a dock/pier, from a float tube or with a long pole from shore. Pick a target area with a known structure or habitat that is likely to hold bluegill and work it until it is completely explored. Good areas to try this technique are next to vertical wood such as docks, piers and standing submerged trees. Good baits are jigs, live bait, ice fishing jigs and blades, to name a few. Different actions can be imparted to the bait such as jigging, dead sticking or a sweep up and drop. Once a fish is encountered try to return to that exact level as that is where they are holding. Vertical fishing can be used to fully probe an underwater structure such as a deadfall to catch every bluegill holding within that structure.

Trolling and Drifting

Trolling is pulling bait rig behind your boat as you move slowly through an area likely to hold bluegills. A jig or heavier crank bait is usually the best tool for the job to get it down to the depth of choice and keep it there while moving at speed. Light powered rods have good backbone to support the weight of the bait rig without completely doubling over as you travel forward making bites easier to detect.

Speed and depth are the two factors that are controlled as you move along. Usually a top speed of 1 to 2 mph is all the faster you will want to go as bluegill may chase a bait a short distance but will give up the goat if the bait is moving too fast and the chase lasts too long. A handheld GPS unit is perfect to track your speed as visual cues are sometimes hard to find out on the water and sometimes ½ of a mph can be the difference between fish and no fish. A trolling motor or paddle can be employed to move you silently along at the right speed but even better is using the wind to your advantage. Moving upwind of an area of interest and then drifting through silently under wind power is very stealthy and allows you to concentrate completely on your fishing with only minor adjustments being needed from the motor or paddle. Occasional jigging or sweeps with the rod can trigger bites by emulating an attempted escape by the bait. In time, bluegills will follow but not bite until they feel an escape is being attempted and only then will they attack.

Investigate a variety of depths when you first hit the water to determine where they are holding. Once a fish is encountered, others in that pond will be close to that same depth in most areas. Remember that bluegills are generally shallow water fish but open water will make them more anxious and they will move deeper to feel more secure. I have found that in many different bodies of water they will gravitate to the 6 to 8 foot range. It doesn't always hold true, but is a very good place to begin your search.

Trolling is the best technique to employ when fishing the open water, deep weed lines and deep submerged structure when fish are active. I have caught many of my biggest bluegill using this method and strongly recommend you giving it a try.

Bottom Dragging

I first learned this technique when fishing for bass and have since found it very productive for bluegill as well. No splitting the atom here, just slowly drag your jig or crank bait across the bottom of the pond with or without jigging. This will cause the bait to kick up bottom sediment and bounce off of structures which creates a racket that gets the attention of any bluegill in the area. It appears to be a fry, crustacean or insect digging in the soft pond bottom foraging and distracted. This makes for a very tempting easy meal for any bluegill and will produce strikes. Bottom areas such as mud flats and sandbars just adjacent to weed lines are good areas to use this technique as there is little risk of snagging and the proper bottom composition to stir up sediments. Fishing this location will cover both the open water bluegill and any just inside the weed line waiting for a meal to pass by. This technique is especially effective for the Redear, who spends their lives focused on bottom dwelling creatures like snails.

Dead Sticking

Dead sticking is a term I borrowed from ice fishing, but it applies to this technique so well that I couldn't think of a better way to describe the action. In this method you are striving for absolutely no movement. You want to hold your bait in front of the nose of the bluegill to let them get a really good look at what you are offering.

This works best with live or prepared bait as the bluegill is going to have plenty of time to inspect and smell what they are about to eat. Inactive fish can be tempted to bite with this method as they will not have to exert any energy to get their meal. An ultra-light rod works well here but you must keep an eye on the rod as the tip will quiver and bend from a light bite before you feel the resistance of the fish. Also keep an eye on the line as they will sometimes strike it as they move up in the water. This will be indicated by the line suddenly becoming slack.

Shooting a Bait

Shooting a dock is a method of getting your bait into an area, but is so useful I felt it needed mentioning. To get your bait into a tight area you can shoot it there by following these steps:

1. Open the bail and secure the line with your finger as if casting
2. Grip the hook at the bend behind the point with your free hand
3. Pull the bait rig back so that it bends the rod loading it with energy
4. Point the rod to where you want the bait to go with the rod
5. Release the hook and quickly release the line so the bait rig slingshots into the target area

This will take some practice to get comfortable with this method but it can come in very handy. Using this casting method you will be able to get your bait rig into spots you could never reach with any other casting methods. Casting into docks, culverts and under overhanging trees are a few places that you will be able to reach with this technique that few, if any, other anglers in the area are capable of reaching.

Countdown Method

The countdown method is a means to get your bait rig back to the same depth where the fish have been located in a consistent manner. I use this mostly while jig fishing but it can be employed for any sinking bait. A bait rig will fall at the same rate in the water each time it is cast out. When the bait rig hits the surface of the water, start counting and begin your retrieval at a 2 count with the first cast, then 4, then 6 and so on. You are in effect fishing the entire water column a slice at a time. When you encounter a fish, you just count back down to that depth because that is most likely the depth the fish are holding. Using this method can help you reproduce a bite and catch more fish quicker.

Fly Fishing Techniques

While casting gets all of the attention in fly fishing, it is really a small part of the process. For every second your fly is in the air, it is not in the right place to catch fish, which is the water. So keep your cast as simple as possible to keep your fly on or in the water for as long as possible. The two casts you need to learn are the basic overhead cast and the roll cast. These are two very efficient casts that get the fly where you want it quickly so you can start fishing and will cover you in most situations. The basic cast is a back and forth motion over your head to get the line up and back down quickly. It is good for open areas and low wind conditions. The roll cast is more of a backup cast for when you are in tight areas or the wind is knocking down the line. Remember that you are casting the line when fly fishing; not the bait. It is a more smooth and gentle action than casting a jig using spinning gear. Don't muscle the rod, but rather move it through the air.

Bringing in the fly is pretty straight forward as well. Slight variations will change the action of the fly and should be considered when using different flies in various situations. Stripping the line gives the fly a fast action followed by a pause where the bite usually takes place. It is accomplished by pulling 3 to 12 inches of line in at a time with your free hand and then pinching it to secure the line with your rod-holding hand while reaching ahead to strip more line. The wrist twist is a slower retrieve that imparts a more erratic movement for the fly. It is performed by pinching the line with the forefinger and thumb, extending the other three fingers toward the rod tip and rotating the wrist to sweep the line with the pinky as it is brought back toward your belly button. Release the line and quickly pinch it again, as the main line will again be close to where you released the last line. Instead of the quick darts of the stripping technique, the wrist roll will give a slower swimming motion.

Ice Fishing

Ice fishing is vertical fishing through a hole in the ice. Actions given to the bait are limited to jigging, dead sticking, larger sweeping actions, stepping the bait up through the water column and slowly swimming straight up. Generally slower techniques work best in the winter as bluegills are going to move minimally to obtain their food to save energy during the hard times of this season.

Catching Big Bluegill

Catching big bluegill is the same process as catching their smaller cousins with the only modification being to focus on areas and waters where these big ones are more likely to be located. By focusing on these areas we are stacking the deck in our favor that the bluegills we encounter will be the bigger size that gets your heart pumping and a smile on your face.

Gathering Intelligence

Before we even think of heading out to catch a bluegill over 10 inches in length, we have to do a little preliminary work. Network and check with every source available including fishing buddies, bait shops, online groups and any other source you can think of contacting. Any and all information you can gather is very useful, from day-to-day information such as what depth they are holding and the colors that are working, to more-to-the-point facts such as stories of people catching large bluegills in a certain area or pond. Most anglers like to think themselves the ultimate poker player never giving away their tricks of the trade, but with some polite conversation you can learn a good amount. Try not to interrogate your friends and sources and be willing to give up some of your personal information in return for theirs. It takes something to get something, so be ready to pony up some of what you know when the time is right and don't be afraid to give out some of your "secrets". I have found that even when you tell a person exactly how, when and where to catch big bluegill, they rarely ever follow that advice and generally don't catch the numbers or size that you will enjoy for a number of reasons.

Also, fortunately for us, many people are more giving when it comes to bluegill. They may closely guard their favorite walleye and bass locations while freely giving away information about bluegill because they have the perception that all bluegill waters are created equally. We know better and can offer information on their favorite quarry in exchange for this bluegill information. Many times you will catch a few of the other species while bluegill fishing, so make a mental note of the particulars and freely share with other anglers in exchange for bluegill specific information.

Big Bluegill Waters

Not all waters that hold bluegill are created equally. Some waters have too much or too little predation and angler pressure, some have just not been stocked with the correct mix of species and others are not fertile enough to grow big bluegills. The best way to determine the quality of bluegills in a pond or lake is to go fishing. I know, life is tough, but it is the best method to tell us what we need to know. Are there bluegills in the water and how big are they? The length, girth and numbers of bluegill and other species caught should be noted. A notebook to record your observations right after getting off the water can be very helpful. It serves as a permanent record that you can refer to instead of completely relying on memory, which has a tendency to get foggy over time. Also, it lets you keep track of several bodies of water at the same time without any confusion.

If a pond has nothing but small fish, it may indicate an over abundance in terms of numbers of bluegill. Bluegill will reach a point where they only grow to a size at which the food supply will support them. It is a self preservation mechanism that allows them to continue the species even in tough times. This could be due to under predation, including fishing pressure, or nutrient poor water. Nutrient poor water will not support enough prey items for the bluegills to feed properly to grow. If the pond has rooted aquatic plants and algae, it probably has enough nutrients as most waters do. Harvesting large numbers of bluegill will change the population over time and allow enough food for some to grow large. If you own the pond, adding predator fish will also reduce the competition for food by reducing the number of mouths that need fed. Stunted bass typically mean good sized bluegills are present. A the bass devour most of the small bluegills this allows the few bluegills that survive to have much more food available and grow to enormous sizes which the small bass cannot eat.

A catch that includes healthy bluegills of all sizes indicates a balanced healthy population. There is enough predator and fishing pressure to remove at least some of the feeding pressure on the population while allowing some to grow to a larger size with the food present. Go ahead and harvest some of your catch in these ponds but try to release at least some of the bigger bluegills. Releasing some of the larger bluegills keeps the genetic pool diverse and includes a predisposition for big bluegills. The big males keep the smaller bluegills off the nesting beds so they focus on eating and growing bigger instead of mating, which makes the population healthier and larger overall. It has been seen in some ponds where only the biggest bluegills are removed that there is a genetic shift to produce only small bluegills. Consider it an angler induced evolution where the "natural selection" process rewards the bluegills with a smaller body size thus pushing the genetics in that direction. It is usually not a problem with a bluegill population but should be considered.

Lastly, we have the prime bluegill pond. This is a pond where the natural predatory pressure is high but angling pressure is low for big bluegill. You will often find this where bass guys are trying to create a giant bass population. The natural predators remove almost all of the small and mid-sized bluegill leaving the large ones with an over abundant food supply. With very little predator pressure and no limit to their food source, they can get enormous. This situation usually does not last long and you should take advantage of it when you find a pond in this state. Unless the bass guys are supplementing the bass' diet with fish chow they will eventually experience a fish kill as the bass starve from lack of prey to eat. Moderate harvesting is recommended here as there are very few new bluegills making it through to replace these big bluegills, BUT these big bluegills will eventually die of old age anyway so better to harvest instead of letting them go to waste.

It is important to keep track of what you are catching one way or another so you know where each fishing location stacks up in producing large bluegills. Never give up on a body of water as conditions may change and it may produce a giant from time to time. Best to check back every few months or at least once a year just to make sure you know what is happening there and that something hasn't shifted the population to producing giants.

Working the Water

Now that we have selected a good pond and know a little about it, let's start working the water to find fish. But where does an angler start? WEEDS! Hopefully you have picked up the fact that bluegills prefer living in and around aquatic plant cover by now. So weeds are a logical place to begin our search for bluegill. Consider the time of year and temperature of the water to choose what depth to begin and the technique to use. Keep moving, but not as fast as those bass guys. You have smaller bait rigs on your line and it will take longer for them to fall. Also, bluegills typically prefer a slower presentation so they can inspect the offering before committing to bite. Work outside weed edges, inside weed edges and any compound structure that involves weeds. After you have fully exhausted the weeds, move onto wood. The next most preferred structure a bluegill will relate to, they will hold tight to that structure so you will have to cast close and probe thoroughly. Keep expanding out from these initial structures until you encounter bluegill.

While targeting these areas, pay attention to the water quality and weather conditions. Once bluegills are encountered, note the specifics such as depth, bait rig that worked, color of that bait, and the action that was being used when the fish bit. A pattern will start to emerge and you can zero in on what is working that day. Once the pattern is figured out, you have the option of continuing on to catch high numbers or tweaking the presentation to go for the big bluegills. Up-sizing your bait and moving out from shore will usually increase your odds of catching the big bluegills. As we know from the life cycle of the bluegill, they start their lives close to shore and cover while young and small and eventually move out into deeper more open areas as they grow larger. Keep refining your presentation and pushing the edges of the deeper water to find the biggest bluegills in the pond.

Let's Go Fishing!

You are now what some would call armed and dangerous. You know about the bluegill: where it lives, what it eats and seasonal habits. You know the proper tackle and bait to utilize to pursue this fish and techniques to employ with those bait rigs. And finally you know how to find, evaluate and fish waters to zero in on locations that hold big bluegill.

Now comes the most important part to catching big bluegill, going out and putting what you know to practice. If you are new to bluegill fishing the learning curve will be steep but fun as you get used to the entire process. For more experienced anglers, it may be a simple matter of slight alterations to what you have done in the past to make yourself more successful on each outing.

Try to learn something each and every time you go bluegill fishing. Nature is wonderful in that it is always changing and never follows our rules. Seasons change, predator and angling pressure change, water quality and levels fluctuate, and so on. I recommend using a ledger to record what works in all of these different conditions on each of your fishing trips. You don't have to write 12 page entries or go into dramatic detail unless you want. The simple fact of putting pen to paper is enough to make many facts stick that would otherwise be forgotten. Put it all into one journal or create separate notebooks for each body of water you fish. Tailor your method to however you can process the information best.

Most importantly, have fun! This should not be a chore, or an overly serious endeavor. Hopefully there is a smile on your face when you head out, while you are on the water and when you return home, no matter the result. Fishing is called that for a reason. If we could guarantee success each time out it would be called catching and would be very boring. Sometimes you will do everything perfectly but they just won't bite. And that is OK! Good luck, and I will see you on the water.

Made in the USA
Monee, IL
23 December 2023